Strategic Language Learning

PEFC

PEFC/16-33-111
CATG-PEFC-052
www.pefc.org

SECOND LANGUAGE ACQUISITION
Series Editor: David Singleton, *Trinity College, Dublin, Ireland*

This series brings together titles dealing with a variety of aspects of language acquisition and processing in situations where a language or languages other than the native language is involved. Second language is thus interpreted in its broadest possible sense. The volumes included in the series all offer in their different ways: on the one hand, exposition and discussion of empirical findings and, on the other, some degree of theoretical reflection. In this latter connection, no particular theoretical stance is privileged in the series; nor is any relevant perspective – sociolinguistic, psycholinguistic, neurolinguistic, etc. – deemed out of place. The intended readership of the series includes final-year undergraduates working on second language acquisition projects, postgraduate students involved in second language acquisition research and researchers and teachers in general whose interests include a second language acquisition component.

Full details of all the books in this series and of all our other publications can be found on http://www.multilingual-matters.com, or by writing to Multilingual Matters, St Nicholas House, 31–34 High Street, Bristol, BS1 2AW, UK.

SECOND LANGUAGE ACQUISITION
Series Editor: David Singleton

Strategic Language Learning
The Roles of Agency and Context

Xuesong (Andy) Gao

MULTILINGUAL MATTERS
Bristol • Buffalo • Toronto

Library of Congress Cataloging in Publication Data
A catalog record for this book is available from the Library of Congress.
Gao, Xuesong.
Strategic Language Learning: The Roles of Agency and Context/Xuesong (Andy) Gao.
Second Language Acquisition: 49
Includes bibliographical references and index.
1. English language--Study and teaching (Higher)--Chinese speakers. 2. English
language--Study and teaching (Higher)--China. 3. Second language acquisition--
Methodology. 4. English language--Acquisition--Methodology. I. Title.
PE1068.C5G36 2010
420.71'151--dc22   2009052775

British Library Cataloguing in Publication Data
A catalogue entry for this book is available from the British Library.

ISBN-13: 978-1-84769-244-2 (hbk)
ISBN-13: 978-1-84769-243-6 (pbk)

Multilingual Matters
UK: St Nicholas House, 31–34 High Street, Bristol, BS1 2AW, UK.
USA: UTP, 2250 Military Road, Tonawanda, NY 14150, USA.
Canada: UTP, 5201 Dufferin Street, North York, Ontario, M3H 5T8, Canada.

The policy of Multilingual Matters/Channel View Publications is to use papers
that are natural, renewable and recyclable products, made from wood grown in
sustainable forests. In the manufacturing process of our books, and to further
support our policy, preference is given to printers that have FSC and PEFC Chain
of Custody certification. The FSC and/or PEFC logos will appear on those books
where full certification has been granted to the printer concerned.

Typeset by Techset Composition Ltd., Salisbury, UK.
Printed and bound in Great Britain by MPG Books Ltd.

To Tong Mankei (Maggie)

Whatever presentation of the activity of many men or of an individual we may consider, we always regard it as the result partly of man's freewill and partly of the law of inevitability.
(Leo Tolstoy in *War and Peace*)

If you know the enemy and know yourself, you will not be in danger in a hundred battles.
If you know the Heaven and you know the Ground, the victory is complete.
(Sun Tzu in *Art of War*)

Contents

Figures and Tables

Figures

Tables

Acknowledgements

I owe a great debt of gratitude to the students who participated in the research, in particular, those who were involved in the longitudinal research phase. Without them, this book would not have been possible.

Many individuals have also helped shape and develop ideas contained in this book, whose contributions should not go unacknowledged. I would like to thank Professor Steve Andrews, Professor Chris Davison, Dr Agnes Lam, Professor David Nunan, and Professor Peter Kelly for their constructive feedback on my research and earlier drafts of the manuscript. I would also like to thank Professor Phil Benson, Professor Andrew Cohen, Dr Brian Morgan, Dr Jing Huang, Dr Wenfeng Wang and my former colleagues at the University of Hong Kong for the intellectual stimuli during the research and writing process. I am also deeply indebted to Professor David Singleton for being a supportive and conscientious editor, without whose encouragement, I shall not see the book in print.

Chapter 1
Introduction

This book reports on an inquiry, conducted in three phases, exploring mainland Chinese students' language learning experiences with a focus on their shifting strategy use prior to and after their arrival in an English-medium university in Hong Kong. The inquiry was motivated by my personal experiences as one of thousands of students moving from the Chinese mainland abroad to pursue tertiary education in English. Like many others, I faced daunting linguistic and academic challenges as a postgraduate student in English-medium universities or study programmes in the United Kingdom, Belgium and Hong Kong. I therefore became interested in understanding the experiences of students like me.

Although I initially intended to find out how mainland Chinese students coped with these challenges in British universities (Gao, 2003, 2006a), my educational experiences in Belgium and Hong Kong have led me to undertake inquiries into another group of Chinese students' language learning experiences (Gao, 2006b, 2008a; Gao *et al.*, 2008). Unlike their counterparts in British, North American or Australian universities, they do their academic studies through the medium of English in multilingual settings, where English may be a less frequently used language. Nevertheless, they still need to develop English competence for their survival and success in the new learning contexts because in these settings English is often a socially important language. In the case of Hong Kong, Cantonese, a regional version of Chinese, functions as the major medium for socialization in daily life and in most social, cultural and political occasions, while English is one of its official languages and widely used in the business and professional sectors. In addition, Putonghua, or Mandarin, the variety of Chinese spoken on the Chinese mainland, is a language of rising importance due to Hong Kong's increasingly economic, socio-cultural and political ties with the mainland since 1997. Thus, Hong Kong presents itself as an interesting setting for an inquiry into learners'

1

strategic learning efforts in order to gain insights into their pursuit of linguistic competence in a multilingual setting.

At the outset of the inquiry, it was noted that language learners tend to be advised to be efficient language learners in terms of strategy use in many learner development programmes due to a popular belief in the importance of strategy use for language learners' learning success (Chamot, 2001; Cohen, 1998; Dörnyei, 2005; Ellis, 1994, 2004; Hsiao & Oxford, 2002; McDonough, 1999; Wenden, 1987, 1998, 2002; Zhang, 2003). In recent decades, the belief in learners' strategy use as a significant cause of variation in their language learning achievements, confirmed by many studies, has given rise to an explosion of research on language learning strategy (LLS). However, it has also attracted many criticisms, such as the under-theorization of the construct itself (Dörnyei & Skehan, 2003; Ellis, 1994; Macaro, 2006) and methodological inappropriateness in LLS research (Dörnyei, 2005; Tseng *et al.*, 2006; for a recent overview of criticisms of LLS research, see Macaro & Erler, 2008), leading to the possible marginalization of LLS research in mainstream language learning research. Moreover, the emphasis on the cognitive and metacognitive aspects of language learning in LLS research has also become problematic as language learning researchers have become increasingly cognizant of the importance of sociocultural contexts in learners' learning (Atkinson, 2002; Block, 2003; Lantolf & Thorne, 2006; Norton Peirce, 1995; Norton & Toohey, 2001; Sealey & Carter, 2004; Watson-Gegeo, 2004; Zuengler & Miller, 2006). This has made it possible to introduce sociocultural perspectives, rarely pursued in LLS research, into research on language learners' strategy use in particular settings (Donato & McCormick, 1994; Oxford, 2003; Palfreyman, 2003; Parks & Raymond, 2004).

Overview of the Inquiry

Drawing on a sociocultural language learning research perspective, the inquiry aimed to understand mainland Chinese undergraduates' language learning experiences and strategy use in an English-medium university in Hong Kong. It addressed the following questions:

(1) To what extent and in what ways does mainland undergraduates' LLS use change during their stay in Hong Kong?
(2) What does this reveal about the relationship between strategy use and context?

'Strategy use' in the above research questions refers to language learners' efforts directed towards success in language learning and/or use (Cohen, 1998). Cohen (1998: 4) further states that 'the element of choice' is a

Table 1.1 An outline of the inquiry

Research	Research methods	Number of participants	Remarks
1st Study (Phase): Baseline (August–September 2004)	Biographical interviews	22	21 interviews transcribed
2nd Study: Follow-up phase (August 2004 to July 2006)	Longitudinal ethnographic-like methods	6	Two dropped out after one year's participation. Another one left Hong Kong for exchange
3rd Study (Phase): Exit (April–July 2006)	Biographical interviews and questionnaires	15	Including six longitudinal study participants

defining characteristic of strategic learning behaviour. Thus, strategy use is related to learners' exercise of agency as it reveals their self-consciousness, reflexivity, intentionality, cognition, emotionality and so on (Carter & New, 2004; Giddens, 1984; Sealey & Carter, 2004). While research to date has usually associated learners' strategy use with cognitive and metacognitive processes (Chamot, 2004; Dörnyei, 2005; Macaro, 2006; Oxford, 2003), the inquiry relates strategy use to learners' broader behavioural engagement in acquiring linguistic competence (Deckert, 2006). Consequently, in this book terms like strategic learning efforts are used interchangeably to refer to learners' strategy use.

The inquiry was conducted in three phases, lasting for two years (Table 1.1). The study in Phase 1 dealt with the questions related to the study participants' strategy use on the Chinese mainland. The study in Phase 2, a longitudinal follow-up phase, focused on six case study participants' language learning experiences and shifting strategy use in Hong Kong. The study in Phase 3 involved the same participants as those in Phase 1 and explored their strategic learning efforts in Hong Kong. Such a design aimed to examine the participants' shifting strategy use both as a group and as individuals.

Methodological Approach

The inquiry, which aimed to achieve a rich and contextualized picture of learners' strategy use, resembles a longitudinal ethnographic-like research approach. Rooted in anthropological research, ethnography has been a long-standing research methodology in the social sciences, including education and sociology (Case, 2004; Cohen *et al.*, 2000; Harkalau, 2005; Pole & Morrison, 2003; Ramanathan & Atkinson, 1999; Richards, 2003; Watson-Gegeo, 1988). Ethnography is 'an approach to social research based on the first-hand experience of social action within a discrete location, in which the objective is to collect data which will convey the subjective reality of the lived experience of those who inhabit that location' (Pole & Morrison, 2003: 16). Traditional ethnography emphasizes the study of cultural behaviour in groups, although most ethnography studies start with individuals (Watson-Gegeo, 1988). It also values an insider perspective and usually requires the researcher to have an extended engagement with research participants in order to obtain a 'thick description' and holistic understanding of the phenomenon under research (Geertz, 1973, 1988; Skyrme, 2007). As a result, ethnographic research tends to be longitudinal in nature. Nevertheless, the ethnographic approach adopted in this inquiry should not be equated with full-scale ethnographies aiming to 'convey the subjective reality of the lived experience' of particular groups of individuals (learners) (Pole & Morrison, 2003: 16); it is best described as 'ethnographic', in line with Ramanathan and Atkinson (1999) who argue that 'ethnographic' research bears features of the full-scale ethnographies defined as above but can be distinguished from them by their narrower focus. In the inquiry, I studied and worked with the participants on campus for two years and even lived with one of the longitudinal phase participants in the same student residential hall for a year. In this manner, I gained first-hand experience and knowledge of the setting where the participants' language learning took place.

The inquiry was also informed by a sociocultural perspective on language learning (Norton & Toohey, 2001; Sealey & Carter, 2004; Zuengler & Miller, 2006). The use of the sociocultural perspective was not intended to be restrictive, but rather operated as 'a well-established fieldwork tradition, a strong conceptual orientation, or a trustworthy sense of intuition' to guide my data collection and analysis in the actual research (Wolcott, 1995: 108). It also helped me to focus on gathering data broadly relevant to my research issues and facilitated my treatment of unstructured data, providing an organizing and sorting structure when analysing the data (Erickson, 2004; Smeyers & Verhesschen, 2001). Far more significantly, it gave me a 'plot' to construct the research narratives contained in this book (Polkinghorne, 1995; Smeyers & Verhesschen, 2001).

The longitudinal nature of the inquiry had an inevitable impact on the research process. Firstly, it was difficult for me to ensure that the number of research participants remained stable throughout the whole inquiry while the small number of participants in the longitudinal follow-up study might limit the generalization of the findings. However, in-depth analysis of the research participants' experiences allows 'analytic generalization' to take place as the participants' experiences were used to 'illustrate, represent, or generalize to a theory' (Yin, 1994: 44). Secondly, as the research moved on, the participants developed their own ideas about the research and reassessed its relevance to them. It was therefore necessary for me to negotiate and re-negotiate with the participants about the forms of the research. Thirdly, as a qualitative researcher constantly in the process of examining and interpreting collected data, I was open to and prepared for new but related research questions to answer and to deal with alternative but relevant research issues as part of the continuous research process. Therefore, although I had a theoretical perspective to guide my research, I also let my data collection and data interpretation evolve as informed by the shifting research reality. For instance, I stopped using a strategy use checklist after negotiating with the research participants in the longitudinal follow-up study. In other words, the methodological approach in this study has certain features of methodological 'bricolage' (Kincheloe & Berry, 2004).

Enhancing Trustworthiness

As a reflexive researcher, I was aware that my position in the research process was never neutral, objective and distant. Instead, my research activities, like the engagement of researchers with the social world, as argued by Bhaskar (1979, cited in Corson, 1991: 233), 'always and necessarily [consist] in a semantic, moral and political intervention in the life of the world, in ways that condition, mediate and transform each other continually'.

In order to retain the involvement of the participants in the longitudinal research process, I also tried to ensure that there were mutual benefits to the participants (Harrison *et al.*, 2001; Sonali, 2006). Regular unstructured interviews or conversations were used to provide the participants with opportunities to use English with a relatively proficient English speaker. In addition, I offered extra help to the participants, such as proofreading their cover letters, resumes and essays. I invariably listened to their struggles in learning English and Cantonese with an empathetic ear. Sometimes I shared with them my own overseas language learning experiences and vulnerability as a non-native speaker teacher in the university. The participants gradually accepted me as a friend. In our conversations,

I witnessed two participants burst into tears when academic and language learning experiences at the university became particularly stressful. Such mutual sharing might have influenced the participants' language learning and had an impact on the research findings. However, 'friendship' can also be considered an important way of obtaining reliable data from the participants (Tillman-Healy, 2003). Nevertheless, I did act as one of many social agents in the context of who mediated the participants' language learning. Consequently, I took extra care to ensure that the findings from this research stage were trustworthy.

In Phases 1 and 3, before I interviewed the participants each time, I explained the purposes of my research and informed them of their rights as research participants in the study. In Phase 2, I largely relied on ongoing reflections on the data and preliminary interpretations and regular attempts to clarify meanings of the data from the participants (Cho & Trent, 2006; Merriam, 1988; Strauss & Corbin, 1998). Firstly, I kept a research journal at the start of the research stage, which recorded my experiences as a non-local resident at an undergraduate residence hall, observations and preliminary interpretations of the data. In order to undertake observation of the participants, I spent a year and a half living in an undergraduate hall, which enabled me to appreciate what it was like to live like a mainland Chinese student among local students. The conversations I had with local and non-local students at the hall of residence helped me to construct and interpret the case study participants' language learning experiences with a focus on their strategy use. I constantly contrasted my own experiences with those of the participants and attempted to relive what they had lived.

Among the many steps I took to enhance the trustworthiness of the research findings, one of the most important things I did was directly put forward some of my initial understandings and impressions to the participants for confirmation or clarification in our regular conversations. During the data collection in Phase 1, I tried to meet all the participants on social occasions such as for lunch to seek clarification related to their interview accounts. I asked them to check and confirm the interview transcripts after interviews were transcribed (Krefting, 1991). When I interviewed 15 of the original 22 participants, including six longitudinal study participants, in Phase 3, I again confirmed my initial findings with them. In the longitudinal research phase, I made repeated attempts to focus some part of the regular conversations on language learning, which helped me to reflect on the different accounts that the participants produced on similar topics at different times. These attempts also helped my critical reading of different accounts and my assessment of how changing life circumstances impacted on the participants' storytelling and how as language learners they had evolved, particularly in terms of strategy use.

With the above-mentioned steps, my involvement enabled me to go more deeply into the participants' language learning experiences in Hong Kong without undermining the trustworthiness of the findings contained in the book.

Organization of the Book

This book consists of seven chapters. Chapter 2 briefly reviews LLS research and then puts forward an argument for adopting a sociocultural perspective in LLS research. As there are many reviews of LLS research, this review does not duplicate such efforts. Rather, it aims to situate socio-cultural LLS research in the context of shifting language learning research paradigms and an increasingly problematized field of LLS research. It also introduces the research framework that guided the inquiry and data analysis. Chapter 3 presents contextual conditions on the Chinese mainland and Hong Kong. The chapter describes how mainland Chinese students came to Hong Kong and what kind of challenges they faced.

Chapter 4 presents findings about the research participants' strategy use in acquiring English on the Chinese mainland from the study conducted in Phase 1. The focus of the chapter is to create a picture of how various social agents mediated the participants' language learning process on the Chinese mainland through the use of cultural artefacts and sociocultural discourses, highlighting the interaction of learner choice and contextual conditions underlying their strategy use.

Chapter 5 looks into the participants' shifting strategy use and its underlying processes in Hong Kong using experiential accounts collected from Phase 3. Before a description is given of the study and its findings, the participants' perceptions of Hong Kong are summarized to set the scene. Then it is demonstrated how contextual conditions mediated the participants' language learning, leading to changes in their strategy use and learning discourses. Chapters 4 and 5 present an overall view of the participants' shifting strategy use as a group in two learning contexts and also illustrate the underlying interaction of agency and contextual conditions.

Chapter 6 goes into more depth, reporting on four case studies drawn from the follow-up study on the participants' learning experiences in Hong Kong in Phase 2. The reporting focuses on the extent to which these individual participants were able to utilize the resources in the learning environment in learning English and how their strategy use was mediated by the existing contextual realities. Together with Chapter 5, Chapter 6 presents a holistic picture of the participants' shifting strategy use and the underlying interaction between agency and contextual conditions.

Chapter 7 concludes with the major findings and insights gained from this study and proposes directions for further research.

Chapter 2

Towards a Sociocultural Perspective on Strategic Learning

As stated in the introductory chapter, this chapter describes and justifies the theoretical perspective that has informed the inquiry. The particular theoretical perspective draws on sociocultural language learning research, which utilizes a variety of approaches to learning, sharing an emphasis on the importance of social, political and cultural processes in mediating learners' cognitive and metacognitive processes (Sealey & Carter, 2004; Thorne, 2005; Zuengler & Miller, 2006). In doing so, I relate the need to have a sociocultural perspective in LLS research to the shifting paradigms in language learning research. In the following sections, I give a short account of LLS research, including the dominant theories, major research methods and problems in the field. Then I go on to explain what the adopted theoretical framework, developed from sociocultural perspectives on language learning, can contribute to LLS research. As language learners' strategy use is seen as resulting from the interaction between agency and contextual conditions in this new perspective, this chapter also examines a variety of positions that can be adopted in the debate of agency and context to inform research on learners' strategic learning efforts.

LLS Research: A Brief Review

In the last three decades, LLS has generated a mass of research from language learning specialists, driven by the assumption that language learning success is at least partially or potentially related to strategy use (Anderson, 2005; Chamot, 2001, 2004; Cohen, 1998; Ellis, 1994, 2004; Griffiths, 2004; Hurd & Lewis, 2008; Macaro, 2006; Oxford, 1989, 1993, 1996; Zhang, 2003). Given the size of the existing LLS research, I do not intend this section to be a comprehensive review but endeavour to highlight as concisely as possible the issues and tensions relevant to this particular study (for comprehensive reviews, see Anderson, 2005; Cohen & Macaro, 2007; McDonough, 1999; Oxford & Crookall, 1989).

Theoretical approaches in LLS research

In one recent review of theoretical conceptions of autonomy, Oxford (2003: 76) conceptualizes context, agency, motivation and learning strategies as integral parts of 'a more systematic and comprehensive theoretical model' of learner autonomy. She also lists five approaches to conceptualizing LLS in research (Table 2.1). Reviews of LLS research indicate that cognitive psychology theories dominate the bulk of LLS research as attested by the definitions of LLS in the field. Wenden (1987: 6) defines LLSs as 'language learning behaviours learners actually engage in to learn and regulate the learning of a second language'. O'Malley and Chamot (1990: 1) regard LLSs as 'the special thoughts and behaviours that individuals use to help them comprehend, learn, or retain new information'. Oxford (1993: 175) considers LLSs 'specific actions, behaviours, steps, or techniques that students employ often consciously to improve

Table 2.1 Learning strategy from different theoretical perspectives

Perspective	*Learning strategies are ...*
Technical	Tools that are 'given' by the teacher to the student through learner training (strategy instruction)
Psychological	Psychological features of the individual features that can change through practice and strategy instruction. Optimal strategy use relates to task, learning style, goals, etc.
Sociocultural I	Clearly implicit in sociocultural theorists' work (e.g. Vygotsky)
Sociocultural II	Learning strategies grow out of the communities of practice. In cognitive apprenticeships, learners gain strategies from expert practitioners. Also learners already have many strategies from their initial communities
Political-critical	Hardly discussed by those who adopt the political-critical perspective, other than to say that they do not belong there. However, learning strategies can help open up access within power structures and cultural alternatives for learners

Source: Adapted from Oxford (2003: 77–79)

their progress in internalizing, storing, retrieving and using the L2'. Cohen (1998: 4) further points out that learning strategies are 'learning processes [...] consciously selected by the learner' with 'the element of choice' giving 'a strategy its special character'. In her review of autonomy theories, Oxford (2003: 81) locates LLSs in two domains, namely behavioural (observable steps) and cognitive (unobservable) processes, and defines strategies as

> specific plans or steps – either observable, such as taking notes or seeking out a conversation partner, or unobservable, such as mentally analysing a word – that L2 learners intentionally employ to improve reception, storage, retention and retrieval of information.

What emerges from these definitions is a portrayal of language learners as 'active mental processors of information and skills' (Chamot *et al.*, 1992: 3) and a picture of language learning as a process whereby learners deal with input and output.

Moreover, LLSs are often represented as 'psychological features that can change through practice and strategy instruction' (Oxford, 2003: 77). However, somewhat paradoxically, despite the assumption that such practice or strategy instruction can occur, individual learners' patterns of strategy use are usually presented as enduring traits. Such conceptions of language learners and language learning have come under scrutiny. Yet criticisms of the theorization of LLS as a psychological trait are not limited to those holding different theoretical perspectives. Even among LLS researchers drawing on cognitive psychology theories, there are a variety of theorizations of LLS and the field has yet to reach a consensus on what constitutes LLSs, especially when conflated with terms such as *tactics*, *skills*, *techniques* and *moves* (Ellis, 1994, 2004; Macaro, 2006; Zhang, 2003). Ellis (1994: 553), in particular notes that '[d]efinitions of learning strategies have tended to be *ad hoc* and atheoretical'. Reviewing definitions of LLS, Dörnyei and Skehan (2003: 611) ask whether LLSs, as an enduring individual difference construct, could be conceived as 'neurological, cognitive, or behavioural processes' (also see Dörnyei, 2005; Tseng *et al.*, 2006).

Development of strategy taxonomies and inventories

In spite of its definitional fuzziness, one of the major contributions made by LLS research 'has been the elaboration of taxonomies, which focus on a range of strategy types', driven by an assumption that 'an understanding of the types of strategies used by good language learners will be [...] beneficial to those who have been less successful' (Parks & Raymond,

2004: 375). Most LLS research has focused on listing, classification and measurement of language learners' strategy use, hoping to establish relationships between learners' strategy use and their learning success (Benson, 2001; Donato & McCormick, 1994; Ellis, 1994; McDonough, 1999). Like the definitions of LLS, there are a variety of strategy taxonomies and inventories in the field and this section discusses only three major ones (see Table 2.2).

Among the three strategy inventories, Oxford (1990) and O'Malley and Chamot (1990) are two of the most influential taxonomies and inventories in the field. O'Malley and Chamot (1990) have 26 strategy items and three categories, namely metacognitive, cognitive and socioaffective strategies, among which the category of socioaffective strategies has three strategy items including questioning for clarification and self-talk. Oxford's (1990) strategy inventory for language learning (SILL) has six categories: cognitive, metacognitive, memory, compensation, social and affective strategies. Strategies in the first three categories of the SILL overlap with the cognitive and metacognitive strategies in O'Malley and Chamot's (1990) inventory, but the SILL appears to have a wider focus and includes strategies associated with the social and affective aspects of language learning and use. Oxford's (1990) SILL has demonstrated great adaptability in strategy research in a variety of academic and independent settings at various educational levels, often in modified and translated forms (Goh & Kwah, 1997; Griffiths, 2003; Huang, 2006; Lan & Oxford, 2003; Mistar, 2001; Nyikos & Oxford, 1993; Oxford & Burry-Stock, 1995; Oxford & Crookall, 1989; Peacock & Ho, 2003).

Cohen *et al.*'s (2006) checklist is a unique list of strategy items as it departs from the traditional emphasis on measuring the frequency of learners' strategy use. It draws on Oxford's SILL and classifies strategy items according to particular language skills, including listening, speaking, writing, reading, vocabulary and translation. It does not ask learners to rate the frequency of their use of particular strategies. Instead, it asks learners to comment on whether they find particular strategies useful and whether they are interested in using new strategies. Therefore, it is not a tool to measure learners' strategy use as a psychological trait but a checklist for them to reflect on the efficacy of their strategy use.

Research methods in LLS research

Most LLS research involves some sort of learners' self-report (Oxford & Burry-Stock, 1995) while other methods, such as observation, have also been used to triangulate interview findings (O'Malley & Chamot, 1990). Based on previous LLS reviews (Cohen, 1998; Gao, 2004; Oxford, 1993;

Table 2.2 Three major strategy inventories and checklists

O'Malley and Chamot (1990)	Three categories (26 items)
	Metacognitive strategies: managing or regulating one's own efforts in the learning process
	Cognitive strategies: related to cognitive processing, such as inferencing, guessing and relating new information to old, etc.
	Socioaffective strategies: how to interact with other learners and manage one's feelings in the learning process. This category only has three items
Oxford (1990)	Six categories (50 items)
	Cognitive strategies: how learners think of their learning
	Metacognitive strategies: how they manage their own learning
	Memory strategies: how learners remember and retain language
	Compensation strategies: how learners make up the limited language to achieve successful language use
	Social strategies: how learners learn language through social interaction
	Affective strategies: how learners adjust their affective status in the learning process
Cohen *et al.* (2006)	This is a skill-specific taxonomy. It has 90 items, in six skill categories including listening, vocabulary, reading, writing, speaking and translation. In each category, strategy items are further divided into strategies for different learning scenarios. In the case of listening strategies, scenarios include 'increase my exposure to new language', 'become familiar with new language' and so on. The checklist, based on this taxonomy, asks language learners to reflect on the efficacy of their strategy use, rather than measure the frequency of their strategy use

Oxford & Burry-Stock, 1995; Oxford & Crookall, 1989), major data collection methods adopted by LLS researchers include the following:

- survey tools or written questionnaires (Ehrman & Oxford, 1989; Fan, 2003; Goh & Kwah, 1997; Gu & Johnson, 1996; Peacock & Ho, 2003; Rao, 2006);

- think-aloud protocols or verbal reports (Block, 1986; Goh, 1998; Lam, 2009; Lawson & Hogben, 1996; Nassaji, 2003);
- interviews (Gan *et al.*, 2004; Gao, 2003, 2006a; Gu, 2003; Li & Munby, 1996; Parks & Raymond, 2004);
- recollective narratives (He, 2002; Oxford *et al.*, 1996);
- diaries or dialogue journals (Carson & Longhini, 2002); and
- observation (O'Malley & Chamot, 1990).

In most LLS research, student-completed, summative rating scales (i.e. survey methods) are the most popular method of data collection for LLS researchers (Bedell & Oxford, 1996; Oxford & Burry-Stock, 1995). The development of strategy taxonomies and inventories has contributed to the increasing use of survey methods in LLS research. According to Ellis (2004: 545), survey studies in LLS research '[allow] a systematic investigation of the various factors that influence strategy use'. However, they also tend to project an ahistoric, decontextualized and static picture of learners' strategy use (Donato & McCormick, 1994; Ellis, 1994; LoCastro, 1994). In contrast, a limited number of qualitative LLS studies, including those of Carson and Longhini (2002) and He (2002), have revealed a much more dynamic picture of learners' strategy use in particular learning contexts.

The work of Carson and Longhini (2002) is a study of Joan Carson's eight-week stay in Argentina, during which she kept a detailed diary of her efforts to learn and use Spanish. Carson completed the SILL on three occasions, at the beginning, middle and end of her stay, and the Style Analysis Survey at the beginning. Her diary entries were also coded for references to strategies and style by Longhini and a colleague. The main findings of the study were based on statistical analysis of these data: Carson's learning style remained relatively constant, but her strategy use varied over the eight-week period, while remaining consistent with her learning style. As another example, He's (2002) autobiographical study of the development of her language learning strategies over the course of her life is divided into six stages: as a teenage English as Foreign Language (EFL) student in pre-Cultural Revolution China, as an independent learner working on an assembly line in a tractor factory during the Cultural Revolution, as a university student after the Cultural Revolution ended, as postgraduate student and a lecturer in Australia, and as a teacher educator in Hong Kong. Relating changes in her strategy use to the demands of each of these contexts, He explains how she mainly used cognitive and metacognitive strategies in school, but made much greater use of metacognitive strategies as an independent learner. A second finding of He's study was that in the early stages of her learning in China she did not consciously select the language learning strategies that she used. Instead, they were acquired in the context of instruction and gradually became automatized. In the later stages of her learning, however, with more exposure to alternative options, she became more conscious of her choice of strategies. Although He emphasizes the ways in which her strategy use changed in response to different contexts of language learning and use, her article conveys a strong sense of her strategy use developing over time and as a consequence of accumulated experience.

Research on learner variation in strategy use

Another major contribution made by LLS research is that the field now has a much more sophisticated understanding of individual differences in learners' strategy use. Research studies have examined in great detail the relationship between learners' strategy use and other individual learner characteristics (Benson, 2001; Benson & Gao, 2008b; Donato & McCormick, 1994; Ellis, 1994; McDonough, 1999).

Reviewing LLS research exploring the relationships between strategy use and individual difference factors, I noted that these learner characteristics could be classified into three categories, innate, acquired and social background, according to the malleability of the characteristics under the influence of context. Learners' *innate characteristics* are those variables such as age, gender (sex), personality and learning styles, which it is assumed they have little control over, were born with or have been socialized into over a long period of time (Ehrman & Oxford, 1989; Goh & Kwah, 1997; Gu, 2003). Learners' *acquired characteristics* are attributes that include motivation, belief and language proficiency, which language learners can effect changes to through conscious and deliberate effort; they have acquired these in the socialization process and these characteristics are subject to dynamic changes in particular contexts (Oxford & Nyikos, 1989; Yang, 1999). Learners' *social background characteristics*, such as study programmes, career choices, institutions and ethnicity, to some degree reflect the features of learning contexts as experienced by language learners, be they the ones that they were born into or chose to affiliate themselves with (Ehrman & Oxford, 1989; Gu, 2003; Oxford & Nyikos, 1989; Peacock & Ho, 2003; Rao, 2006). In these studies, learning strategies, situated on the border of 'context' and 'language learner', are considered 'learner actions', revealing the influences of 'learners' cognitions and their explicit beliefs [. . . and] self-efficacy beliefs' (Ellis, 2004: 544). They connect the contextual processes with inner processes taking place within the learners.

In recent years, strategy researchers have displayed a greater awareness of the necessity to explore strategy use among particular cultural groups of learners in specific sociocultural contexts and/or task settings. The number of such studies is steadily on the increase (for recent studies, see Goh & Kwah, 1997; Gu, 2003; Oxford *et al.*, 2004; Peacock & Ho, 2003; Rao, 2006), but more LLS research is needed to explore learners' contextualized strategy use (Chamot, 2004; Hsiao & Oxford, 2002).

Major criticisms of LLS research

As mentioned earlier, although LLS research has made a major contribution to language learning research, it has also been challenged by both researchers who adopt cognitive approaches to language learning research and those who endorse alternative research perspectives. Most of these criticisms are related to the conceptualization of the construct of LLS and methodological approaches in LLS research (Dörnyei, 2005; Macaro, 2006; Macaro & Erler, 2008). In addition, researchers using sociocultural perspectives call for a more holistic perspective on learners' strategy use by shifting the focus from the learner to the learner-in-the-context.

Firstly, critics find it problematic that LLSs are defined as being both cognitive and behavioural, contending it is often not possible to differentiate between 'an ordinary learning activity and a strategic learning activity' (Dörnyei, 2005: 164). Strategy researchers such as Cohen (1998) assert that 'the element of choice' could be a defining characteristic of strategic learning behaviour. However, Dörnyei (2005: 165) argues that

> students tend to make several choices concerning their learning process that are not strategic in the strict sense, that is, which do not necessarily involve appropriate and purposeful behaviour to enhance the effectiveness of learning.

Tseng *et al.* (2006) propose the use of self-regulatory capacity and self-regulation to replace the construct of LLS and strategic learning so that cognitive and metacognitive mechanisms underlying the behavioural aspect of learners' strategy use can be captured.

Other researchers question the dominance of questionnaires as strategy measurement instruments, arguing that some popular strategy questionnaires can be psychologically flawed because the frequency of individual learners' strategy use measured by these questionnaires cannot be cumulative in representing LLS as a psychological trait (Dörnyei, 2005; Dörnyei & Skehan, 2003). It remains questionable whether these questionnaires 'measure what they purport to measure' and 'do so consistently' (Ellis, 2004: 527).

It is also questionable whether simple strategy questionnaires measure the reality of learners' strategy use in particular contexts (Gao, 2004). Phakiti (2003) points out the problem when the frequency data of learners' strategy use are analysed together with constructs such as gender, which is both biologically static (sex) and socioculturally dynamic (gender). He argues that learners' strategic behaviour is dynamic and, in order to have a proper understanding of their strategy use in relation to many of their individual characteristics, one has to situate their strategy use in specific settings and identify what particular goals or aims these learners use strategies for (also see Macaro, 2006). Phakiti (2003: 681) also contends that learners' self-reported strategy use 'should be seen as [their] stable long-term knowledge of their strategy use'. This indicates a need to explore how individual learners develop appropriate strategy use in response to different learning tasks in particular learning settings across time, while it also questions the postulation in LLS research that successful language learning is at least partially related to the frequency of learners' strategy use.

Researchers using other theoretical orientations, namely sociocultural perspectives on language learning, have come to a similar conclusion from a different angle. Although few in number, sociocultural LLS studies problematize the connection between language learners' performance and their strategy use in the bulk of LLS research (Gillette, 1994; Parks & Raymond, 2004). Parks and Raymond (2004) are critical of the correlation studies on learners' strategy use and other individual factors, such as motivation, as these studies tend to present these attributes as relatively fixed and stable across contexts. They argue that these studies often present strategy use as 'largely [pertaining] to individual will and knowledge' (Parks & Raymond, 2004: 375). If choice is a defining characteristic of learners' strategic learning behaviour (Cohen, 1998), they are concerned to what extent the choice rests with learners or is mediated by the particular social contexts in which learners are engaged. Moreover, they call for a shift in the conceptualization of language learners, learning, context and LLS (Norton & Toohey, 2001; Oxford, 2003), which will be presented in detail in the following sections.

The Shifting Language Learning Research Landscape

In what Block (2003) regards as the 'social turn' in SLA research, sociocultural perspectives have recently become more established in language learning research (Atkinson, 2002; Block, 2003; Ellis, 1994; Lantolf & Thorne, 2006; Littlewood, 2004; Morgan, 2007; Sealey & Carter, 2004; Watson-Gegeo, 2004; Zuengler & Miller, 2006). The landscape of language learning research is now characterized by diversified research foci and increased attention to the sociocultural contexts of language learning (Table 2.3). Cognitive theories of language learning, which have provided the foundations for mainstream SLA research for years, are being challenged by the claim that language learning takes place not just in individual learners' minds but also in society. Terms like community of practice (COP) (Lave & Wenger, 1991; also Wenger, 1998, 2000) are increasingly used in research to describe social networks in which language learners find themselves.

Table 2.3 A simplified contrast between cognitive and sociocultural LLS research

	Cognitive psychological approaches	*Sociocultural perspectives (a political and critical version)*
Context	An immediate material learning setting and an important variable modifying learners' cognition and metacognition	Fundamental to language learning, a combination of material conditions, sociocultural discourses, sociocultural networks and the social relations underlying the alignments and arrangements of various contextual elements
Learners	Autonomous actors processing language-related information and skills	Social beings that have a range of socially constructed elements in their identities and their relationship to learning, such as class, ethnicity and gender. They also have a dynamic, reflexive and constantly changing relationship with the social context of learning
Language learning	Cognitive and metacognitive activities in individual learners' brains	Both a kind of action and a form of belonging
LLSs	Cognitive and metacognitive procedures that enhance the mental processing of language	Learner actions to subvert the contextual conditions for alternative learning opportunities, apart from their role in enhancing the cognitive/metacognitive processes

Source: Based on Mitchell and Myles (1998), Oxford (2003), Palfreyman (2006) and Wenger (1998)

Meanwhile, the social turn is also accompanied by an advance of critical perspectives in language teaching, promoting a shift from 'a preoccupation with language as an *end-in-itself*' to 'a vehicle for self-discovery and social transformation' (Morgan, 2007: 1035, also see Corson, 1991, 1997; Norton & Toohey, 2004). Concepts like power, identity and agency have been given close attention in the works of those who endorse critical and poststructural theories (Corson, 1997; Norton Peirce, 1995; Norton, 2000; Norton & Toohey, 2004; Morgan, 2004, 2007). In doing so, some of these researchers criticize sociocultural perspectives, in particular the view of learning contexts as COPs (e.g. Lave & Wenger, 1991; Wenger, 1998), for 'exaggerating the internal cohesion and cooperation of collectivities and for understating the operation of discourse and power through the communication of group norms' (Morgan, 2007: 1046). Morgan (2007: 1046) also notes that sociocultural and COP research tend to grant 'individuals a degree of autonomy and self-awareness' more than in critical perspectives. He concludes that sociocultural research may be invigorated if combined with more critical approaches. For this reason, this book draws on a more critical version of the sociocultural perspective (Oxford, 2003, also see Table 2.1).

From such a sociocultural perspective, researchers assume that context or real-world situations are 'fundamental, not ancillary, to learning' (Zuengler & Miller, 2006: 37), while in cognitive theories, context tends to be treated as a variable modifying the internal acquisition process occurring in individual minds (Block, 2003; Norton & Toohey, 2001; Sealey & Carter, 2004; Thorne, 2005; Watson-Gegeo, 2004). For this reason, the term 'context' needs some further elaboration and can be defined in a variety of ways. For instance, 'context' may be used to refer to aspects of the immediate physical setting of learners' language learning, for example the classroom. It can also be defined in terms of less tangible forms, namely cultural capital (Bourdieu, 1986) or social capital (Putnam, 2000), underscoring the benefits that individuals can have by possessing certain skills/knowledge or having privileged access to certain social networks (Norton, 2000; Palfreyman, 2006). It may also refer to social relations or the structure underlying the social alignments and arrangements of other contextual elements (Layder, 1990).

Researchers also take this sociocultural perspective to view learners as social agents in active pursuit of language-related competence and non-linguistic objectives (Norton Peirce, 1995; Norton, 2000). In addition, they conceptualize language learning not only as individual metacognitive and cognitive activities but also as social acts that are meaningfully related to learners' identity formation (Norton & Toohey, 2001; Oxford, 2003; Thorne,

2005; Watson-Gegeo, 2004). Thus, language learning in the COP 'combines personal transformation with the evolution of social structures' through learners participating in those communities (Wenger, 2000: 227); it is also 'both a kind of action and a form of belonging' for learners (Wenger, 1998: 4). Such paradigm shifts and theoretical reconceptualizations also help researchers to capture learners' dynamic strategy use in LLS research.

Sociocultural Perspectives and LLS Research

As a result of this shift in the conceptualizations of context, learners and language learning, sociocultural researchers regard learners' strategy use as both a cognitive choice made by individuals and an emergent phenomenon 'directly connected to the practices of cultural groups' (Donato & McCormick, 1994: 453). From this perspective, learners' strategy use can also aim to subvert the imposed learning context to create alternative learning opportunities, and not just facilitate their cognitive and metacognitive learning processes (Norton & Toohey, 2001; Oxford, 2003). Consequently, the emergence of learners' strategy use can be considered closely related to a process of contextual mediation and learners' exercise of agency (Gao, 2008b; Gao & Benson, 2008; Norton & Toohey, 2001; Thorne, 2005; Toohey & Norton, 2003). The following sections look at the nature of sociocultural perspectives on language learning and highlight those components that are of particular relevance to LLS research, including mediation and activity theory. They also focus on the features of research methods in sociocultural language learning inquiries and LLS research.

Sociocultural Perspectives in Language Learning Research

Fundamental to a sociocultural perspective on learners' strategy use is the concept that the 'human mind' is mediated (Lantolf, 2000: 1). The concept of mediation can potentially be used to demonstrate the link between learners' strategy knowledge and their actual strategy use at a macro-level. Human activity, conceived as *tool-mediated goal-directed action* by Zinchenko (1985, cited in Lantolf, 2000: 7, original italics), integrates socially and culturally constructed forms of mediation and provides the basic unit of analysis in the sociocultural framework; this helps researchers to interpret learners' learning behaviour at a micro-level in terms of their goals, roles and means in particular settings (Donato & McCormick, 1994). Therefore, sociocultural LLS research aims to achieve a balanced theorization of agency and context in relation to their explanatory roles in understanding learners' strategy use.

The sociocultural perspective stresses the role of agency in learners' strategy use through its theorization of activity. Human activities, including learners' learning activities, are understood at three levels of abstraction: the level of *activity*, which refers to human behaviour in a general sense and is closely associated with motives, the level of *action*, which is goal-oriented and inseparable from a conscious goal, and the level of *conditions*, under which a goal-oriented action is carried out (Lantolf, 2000; McCafferty *et al.*, 2001). Activity theory emphasizes that specific goal-directed actions, mediated by appropriate means, help individuals to fulfill their motives under particular spatial and temporal conditions (Lantolf, 2000: 8). Therefore, on the one hand, sociocultural perspectives offer frameworks that cut deep into the complexity of human behaviour by examining social contexts where such behaviour takes place (Donato & McCormick, 1994; Lantolf & Appel, 1994; Mitchell & Myles, 1998). On the other hand, they also help shed light on the reality that the same activity can mean different things to individual learners as they pursue different goals. It is agency that underlies the learners' dynamic strategic behaviour as they constantly transform their strategy use to pursue their goals in response to contextual changes.

The concept of mediation highlights the critical importance of context in shaping language learners' strategy use. There are three types of contextual resources that potentially mediate learners' language learning and strategy use, including learning discourses ('discursive resources'), artefacts and material conditions with their associated cultural practices ('material resources'), and social agents ('social resources') (Donato & McCormick, 1994; Palfreyman, 2006). Contextual learning discourses, reflecting the dominant values, attitudes and beliefs attached to learning a foreign language, can cause changes in language learners' discourses about values, attitudes and beliefs in the learning process and, in turn, their strategy use. At the micro-level, learners' discourses empower them to organize and control mental processes, such as selective attention to the environment, planning, articulating steps in the process of solving a problem and so on. At the macro-level, discourses about learning a language reflects the values that learners attach to the target language and goals that they want to achieve through strategy use, while learners' motives or goals are crucial in determining their strategy use (Gillette, 1994; Oxford, 2003).

The availability and accessibility of material and cultural artefacts helps language learners to adopt different strategies from the time when these tools and artefacts are not available or accessible. In mediating learners' strategy use, these artefacts are often associated with various cultural practices in particular contexts. For instance, an English text can be used by teachers in one context in forcing learners to memorize chunks of English. It could also be read by learners for fun in another context. Since all the material and artefacts are activated by other humans to mediate language learners' thinking and strategy use, these mediators or agents are also influential in the development of learners' strategy use. Various social agents' actions not only mediate discourses to language learners but also provide the material support and assistance that are crucial for learners' engagement in acquiring linguistic competence. Language learners interact with these agents for assistance or inspiration in their language learning and strategy use.

In some cases, these contextual resources can be distinguished from each other, but in many others they are often integrated with each other and the distinction between them is somewhat artificial. For instance, a textbook containing a message to encourage students to work hard to learn English can be considered both a piece of motivating discourse and an artefact (part of material learning conditions). Nevertheless, a close look at the three contextual (mediation) sources, namely discursive resources, social agents as well as material conditions and cultural artefacts, is likely to enhance our understanding of the developmental process of learners' strategy use (Donato & McCormick, 1994; Palfreyman, 2003, 2006). The next section will look at two empirical LLS studies that use sociocultural perspectives and examine the mediation of contextual (mediation) sources on learners' strategy use.

Sociocultural Perspectives and Empirical LLS Research

In reviewing sociocultural LLS research, it is noteworthy that sociocultural perspectives, although considered 'robust' in investigating the developmental process of learners' strategy use, have not been widely utilized (Donato & McCormick, 1994: 462). In an exploratory attempt, Donato and McCormick (1994) link learners' shifting strategy use over time with the introduction of a new mode of assessment, namely portfolio assessment. Donato and McCormick (1994: 459) found that their French learners developed their goals in learning and 'identifying a goal is the first step [...] in the genesis of strategic action'. Moreover, resulting from the learners' goal setting and self-assessment, they also became more skilful in adopting specific strategies to achieve particular learning goals. Donato and McCormick (1994) also found that all the participants increased the frequency of strategy use as recorded in their portfolios. They argue that sociocultural LLS research provides a robust framework that can be utilized in explaining learners' strategy development.

Drawing on data from a longitudinal inquiry into a group of Chinese students' participation in an English for Academic Purposes (EAP) course in a North American University, Parks and Raymond (2004: 374) see learners' strategy use as 'a complex, socially situated phenomenon, bound up with [...] personal identity'. They examined how the students' interaction with native speakers had mediated their strategy use in three areas: reading textbooks, attendance at lectures and participation in group work. For instance, the paper observes that one participant (Helen) learnt to use note-take strategies from her Canadian study mates so that she could improve her understanding and recall of textbook materials. Parks and Raymond (2004: 384) further note that learners' 'desire to speak and interact with native speakers may not be totally dependent on the will of the [individuals], on the mere knowledge that social interaction is a good learning strategy', but also on their need to 'reposition themselves' vis-à-vis their interlocutors, namely Canadian students in the learning context'.

In contrast to other LLS research, both Donato and McCormick (1994) and Parks and Raymond (2004) adopted a longitudinal qualitative research approach to capture language learners' sociocultural history and developmental process of strategy use. The longitudinal nature of these inquiries helps researchers to explore how individual learners choose appropriate strategies in response to contextual changes across time and thus to capture their dynamic strategy use. While such research aims to reveal insights into learners' situated strategy use, there are a number of criticisms of sociocultural LLS research that need to be addressed. These will be examined in detail in the next section.

Criticisms of Sociocultural LLS Research

Although giving promise of insights into learners' emerging strategy use in response to contextual mediation, sociocultural LLS research has also been challenged like those studies endorsing other theoretical alternatives. One criticism that has been made is that sociocultural LLS researchers are unable to distinguish findings or research claims from the actual research data (Mitchell & Myles, 1998). Another concern is whether researchers should place the emphasis on learner agency or learning context in learners' strategy development (see Palfreyman, 2003; Wenden, 2002). These criticisms will be dealt with in turn.

On methodological grounds, Mitchell and Myles (1998) criticize sociocultural research for its failure to establish cause–effect relationships between the evidence and their claims. They point out that the

sociocultural approach is beset by the problems associated with interpretative naturalistic research. For instance, Donato and McCormick
(1994) fail to clarify whether the portfolio assessment, which required
their students to document how they learnt, only records development
in the student participants' strategy use or whether it also fosters such
development. The mediation role of portfolio assessment as claimed by
Donato and McCormick (1994) is thus called into question. A possible
solution is proposed by Palfreyman (2003) who suggests that researchers
have a broader research concern, going beyond simply documenting
learning strategies. As a result, the inquiry reported in this book not only
examined learners' learning contexts and language learning experiences,
but also explored social mediation and strategy development. In addition, it developed LLS research in terms of its methodological design by
adopting a multi-method research approach so that the data could be
mined to generate robust research claims.

Another difficulty in adopting a sociocultural approach in LLS research
is in how to reach a careful balance in assessing learner agency and learning context. Wenden (1998, 2002) acknowledges the valuable contributions
that sociocultural research can make to enhance our understanding of language learning. However, she is also critical of the sociocultural theorists'
over-emphasis on the deterministic role of the learning context or setting
in learners' strategy use. She argues that sociocultural LLS researchers,
while recognizing the importance of contextual mediation on learners'
strategy use, tend to ignore the role of learners' beliefs, knowledge or
metacognitive knowledge in their choice of strategy use. Commenting on
studies including those of Gillette (1994) and Coughlan and Duff (1994),
Wenden (1998: 530) reminds readers that:

> In these studies the knowledge/beliefs embedded in the setting or
> which emerge through the interaction that takes place in it is over-
> looked as a source of insight on learner's motives, goals and opera-
> tions. The review, on the role of metacognitive knowledge in the
> self-regulation of learning, highlights this variable that appears to be
> ignored and underdeveloped in sociocultural theory.

In contrast, Palfreyman (2003: 244) warns that, by placing an emphasis on
agency as part of learners' 'personal assets', there is also a danger of rein-
forcing the 'cognitive individual' and divorcing learners from contexts,
thereby presenting an impoverished view of learners.

To address this theoretical difficulty, this book draws on the sociological debate over agency and structure to develop a more refined understanding of these two concepts. In the next section, I will review this debate

in social science research and explain the rationale for adopting a realist solution (Layder, 1990) in sociocultural LLS research.

Structure and Agency in LLS Research

The debate over agency and structure has been an ongoing one in the social sciences (Carter & New, 2004; Giddens, 1984; Layder, 1990; Sealey & Carter, 2004). In this book, the sociological debate has been adapted so that its relevance to sociocultural LLS research could be highlighted. I therefore begin this section with some explanation of the two key terms.

The notion of 'structure' in the original debate concerns social structure, or social relations underlying social and contextual alignment and arrangements, and has more ideological and abstract connotations (Dean *et al.*, 2006; Layder, 1990). It is understood that the more abstract one particular element is, the more difficult it is to capture its interaction with the participants' agency in an empirically straightforward manner. Therefore, in this book, the term 'structure' stands for the tangible contextual elements that are indicative of the social relations underlying their alignments and arrangements. Consequently, the term 'structure' is used together with 'contextual conditions', 'contextual realities' or 'context' to refer to contextual resources that constitute learning contexts and mediate learners' language learning and strategy use, such as materials (artefacts), discourses and social networks (Donato & McCormick, 1994; Palfreyman, 2006).

Agency is related to a human being's self-consciousness, reflexivity, intentionality, cognition, emotionality and so on (Carter & New, 2004; Giddens, 1984; Sealey & Carter, 2004). It is also logically connected to power, another central concept in the social sciences (Giddens, 1982, 1984). To be an agent, who could act *otherwise*, 'is to be able to deploy ... a range of causal powers', which 'is very often defined in terms of intent or the will, as the capacity to achieve desired and intended outcomes' (Giddens, 1984: 14–15). Theorized as such, this view of power encompasses more than mere metacognitive knowledge and self-regulatory capacity. Apart from metacognitive knowledge and self-regulatory learning capacity (or the term 'strategic learning capacity'), language learners also need to have capacities to secure 'the right to speak' and 'the power to impose reception' to their linguistic competence (Norton, 2000: 8; also see Norton & Toohey, 2001; Oxford, 2003; Palfreyman, 2003; Toohey & Norton, 2003). Learners' use of such capacities may involve having an appropriate understanding of contextual conditions and critically identifying contextual elements for possible reconfiguration, which is referred to in this book as

'sociocultural capacity'. It also involves learners' micro-political competence in manipulating contextual conditions and social processes within
particular contexts to create a facilitative learning environment, negotiate
access to language competences and pursue self-assertion in the COP
where language learning takes place.

Moreover, the power of social agents includes their will, their intent or
motives and their beliefs in learning, which can be captured in their language learning narratives. In recounting what they have done in the learning process, they can make their conduct meaningful and strategic because
of their capacity for reflexivity. Because of language learners' agency, their
conduct in the learning process is often goal-oriented, intentionally
invoked and effortful, or strategic. In other words, it is agency that gives
'the element of choice' (Cohen, 1998: 4) to learners' strategy use as a special characteristic. Therefore, on the one hand, learners' self-reported strategy use may be problematic if it is treated as a means of psychometric
measurement (Dörnyei, 2005; LoCastro, 1994; Tseng *et al.*, 2006); on the
other hand, learners' accounts of their strategy use do provide opportunities to explore the interplay of agency and contextual conditions underlying their strategy use.

Four positions in the agency and structure debate

According to Sealey and Carter (2004), there are four major positions in
the debate on individual agency and structure. These positions are the
structuralist position, the voluntarist position, the structuration position
and the realist position.

Figure 2.1 illustrates the structuralist position, which views human
beings as determined by social relations and learners' strategy use as
effects or outcomes of such social relations. Learners' strategy use, their
exercise of power, seems to be negligible in the face of the overwhelming
contextual constraints. The element of choice is often a neglected feature
of learners' behaviour. Research indicative of the structuralist position
involves an examination of the structural elements in particular contexts,
including cultural traditions, in explaining language learners' behaviour.
In the case of Chinese learners, the traditionally defined roles of teacher
and students are often cited as factors causing Chinese students to be less
willing to take their own initiative in learning (Cortazzi & Jin, 1996; Wen &
Clement, 2003). The argument that autonomy may not be culturally
appropriate in particular contexts due to different cultural traditions (Ho &
Crookall, 1995; Jones, 1995) has a ring of the structuralist perspective, in
which the role of structure is emphasized far more than that of agency in
shaping human behaviour and learners' strategy use.

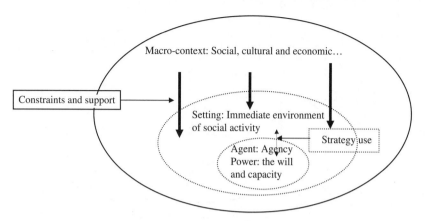

Figure 2.1 A structuralist view (based on Carter & New, 2004; Layder, 1990)

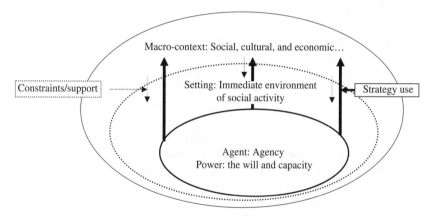

Figure 2.2 A voluntarist view (based on Carter & New, 2004; Layder, 1990)

Figure 2.2 illustrates a voluntarist view of agency and structure. In contrast to the structuralist argument, great emphasis is placed on the role of agency, while the role of contextual conditions in understanding learners' strategic behaviour is marginalized. Contextual conditions are identified as one variable affecting learners' strategy use, with the source of learner actions (strategy use) and 'choice' a product of individual learners' will and knowledge (Parks & Raymond, 2004). Most LLS research, in particular that undertaken from a cognitive psychology perspective, has largely focused on learners' agency in determining strategic efforts (Donato & McCormick, 1994; Norton & Toohey, 2001), although the version of agency in cognitive LLS research is much narrower (Palfreyman, 2003).

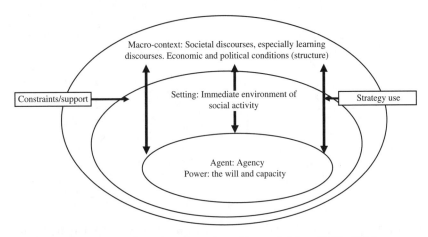

Figure 2.3 A structuration view (based on Carter & New, 2004; Giddens, 1976; Layder, 1990)

Figure 2.3 shows the third position in the structure–agency debate, structuration theory, which attempts to remove the dualism of agency and structure, seeing them as two interdependent constructs produced and reproduced through their mutual interaction (Giddens, 1976, 1982, 1984). Giddens asserts that social structures (rules and resources) 'are both constituted by human agency, and yet at the same time are the very medium of this constitution' (1976: 121). As a result, neither structure nor agency is given primacy in determining human behaviour as they are mutually dependent on each other and have a profound impact on learners' behaviour when activated. The structuration approach in LLS research implies that learners are highly reflexive and knowledgeable agents who are able to provide a clear rationale for their actions and from whose actions social contexts for learning are instantiated. Thus, learners' choice in strategy use is inseparable from structure as the choice itself makes structure. It also recognizes the dynamic nature of learners' agency as agency emerges from its interaction with contextual structure. However, somehow this view under-emphasizes the objective existence of structure and exaggerates learners' capacity to change it and create favourable learning conditions.

Figure 2.4 presents the realist position, which is the position adopted in this book. Realists maintain that agency and structure each have their own distinct autonomous properties while in reality they interact with each other and have emerging properties from such interaction. On the one hand, structure or contextual conditions are always historically anterior to learners and provide an enduring stage for them to act upon. On the other

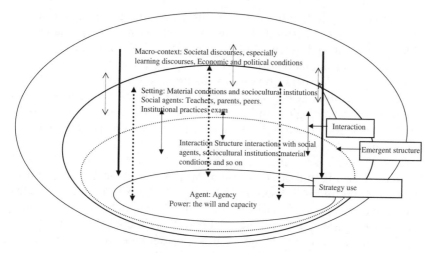

Figure 2.4 A realist view (based on Carter & New, 2004; Layder, 1990)

hand, agency is associated with the use of the power of self-consciousness, reflection, intentionality, cognition and emotionality (Carter & New, 2004; Layder, 1981, 1985, 1990; Sealey & Carter, 2004).

Realists also consider power as a structural property in addition to being a precondition to individual agency (Layder, 1985). Realists argue that, between two extremes of agency and structure, there is a space called 'interaction structure' giving rise to emergent properties due to particular combinations of things, processes and practices (Carter & New, 2004; Layder, 1981). On the one hand, language learners may use particular strategies to add new properties to the existing contextual elements and these new properties gradually become stratified into different layers of contextual conditions. On the other hand, their interaction with contextual elements may empower them with new will and capacity or lead to further constraints on their use of power. Beyond the 'interaction structure', the macro contextual elements and conditions retain their relatively enduring features and their existence does not depend on learners' strategic efforts. However, the realist view does not assume a deterministic view of structure in explaining human behaviour. Realists acknowledge that agency makes it possible for social agents to 'reflect upon' and 'seek to alter or reinforce the fitness of the social arrangements they encounter for the realization of their own interests' (Sealey & Cater, 2004: 11). Meanwhile, social agents' such active interpretation and reconstruction operate within the constraints and supporting features of the contextual conditions that exist independently. In other words, realists recognize that language learners' strategy use is an essentially constrained choice and choice made possible by the context, but nevertheless a learner's choice is still a choice.

This realist position in the debate allows sociocultural LLS researchers to regard language learners' strategy use as the result of a continual interaction between learner agency and context. Moreover, the realist position has important epistemological and methodological implications for researchers. If agency and structure have their own autonomous properties while generating further layers of social realities, LLS research, by adopting this position, requires an empirical inquiry into learners' verbal accounts of language learning and strategy use as well as a technical description of contextual conditions (Corson, 1997; Layder, 1990, 1993). Taking this realist epistemological position, sociocultural strategy researchers need to interpret research participants' experiential narratives in the light of the contextual realities that give rise to them. Such considerations have informed the particular sociocultural framework adopted in this inquiry.

Sociocultural interpretative framework for this study

Drawing on the realist position on agency and structure, this inquiry adapted Layder's (1993) research resource map into an analytical framework (see Figure 2.5) to help explore dynamicity in learners' strategy use in particular contexts. The framework incorporates contextual resources for language learning in sociocultural perspectives and places them in Layder's (1993) research map. The map has four components: context, setting, situated activity and self. 'Context (macro-context)' refers to societal discourses about language learning, the economic situation, inter-group social relationships (e.g. social classes) and political conditions. 'Setting' is the immediate environment for language learning. The setting contains contextual resources [including material, discursive and social resources (Palfreyman, 2006)] that are potentially accessible by language learners. In specific terms, they may refer to physical learning settings, cultural artefacts (examinations), sociocultural institutions (institutional culture), material conditions and so on. The setting also encompasses social relationships between language learners and mediating agents such as teachers, peers and parents in particular institutional settings. 'Situated activity' refers to the interaction between language learners and contextual resources, including mediating agents (social resources) in specific learning settings. 'Self' is learners' self-conceptualization and biographical experiences. 'Self' is also where learner agency and power is located, which includes not only learners' will (motives and beliefs) but also their

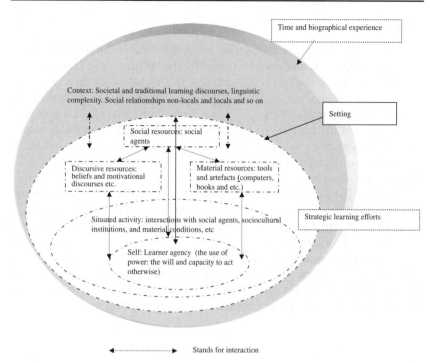

Time and biographical experience

Context: Societal and traditional learning discourses, linguistic complexity. Social relationships non-locals and locals and so on

Setting

Social resources: social agents

Discursive resources: beliefs and motivational discourses etc.

Material resources: tools and artefacts (computers, books and etc.)

Situated activity: interactions with social agents, sociocultural institutions, and material conditions, etc

Strategic learning efforts

Self: Learner agency (the use of power: the will and capacity to act otherwise)

Stands for interaction

Figure 2.5 The analytical framework for the study (adapted from Layder, 1993)

capacities to act in the learning process, such as strategic learning capacity, sociocultural capacity and micro-political capacity.

Figure 2.5 also indicates that a crucial element in this framework is the historical dimension, as four different components of the framework consistently interact with each other, leading to the emergence of temporal contextual reorganization and changes in individual learners' self. In this framework, language learners' accounts of strategy use are theorized as an important means to inquire into the ongoing interaction between language learner (agency) and contextual conditions, including macro-contexts and institutional settings, in a historical perspective. In the light of technical descriptions of learning contexts, learners' shifting strategy use can be accounted for through exploring and interpreting the empirical data relevant to different layers of social realities, from learners themselves to processes including the social relations underlying the arrangements of learning resources and alignments of mediating agents at particular institutional settings.

Conclusion

This chapter has presented a brief account of the existing LLS research and its problems. It has also documented the shifting language learning research landscape before going on to describe how sociocultural perspectives can be utilized in LLS research. In addition, it has discussed the methodological implications of undertaking sociocultural LLS research. Finally, it has attempted to develop a more refined understanding of agency and structure in sociocultural LLS research, which is needed in the exploration of learners' situated strategy use in particular contexts. This chapter has also argued in favour of a careful description of different layers of social realities, including contextual conditions, institutional setting and an individual's biographical experiences in interpreting language learners' language learning and strategy use (Layder, 1993). The particular framework advanced in this chapter has enabled me to acknowledge language learners' capacity to seek and create facilitative learning settings and at the same time to critically examine the contextual mediation of their learning. It has also helped me to explore how learners' strategy use, often as a constrained choice, remains the learners' choice.

Chapter 3

Mainland Chinese Students' Migration to Hong Kong

As was shown in Chapter 2, one of the keys to understanding language learners' strategic learning is to have some knowledge of the learning contexts and, of particular relevance to this inquiry, mainland Chinese students' migration for further studies to Hong Kong. In this chapter, I shall describe the educational and social context on the Chinese mainland to illustrate the contextual forces pushing mainland Chinese students to migrate to other educational contexts in pursuit of English-medium tertiary education. I will also draw on research literature and my personal knowledge to portray the social, linguistic and educational context in Hong Kong. As a mainland Chinese in Hong Kong, I experienced many challenges and difficulties similar to those of many mainland Chinese students.

Education on the Chinese Mainland

Education occupies a central position in the Chinese cultural tradition and has remained a top priority among the concerns felt by most Chinese, despite the dramatic social, cultural and political shifts in China over the centuries (Elman, 2000; Lee, W., 1996; Lee, H., 2000; Miyazaki, 1976; Thøgersen, 2002). Cultural discourses, especially writings by Confucius and on Confucianism, emphasize learning for one's own self or moral perfection and the implication of such individual perfection in social transformation (Bai, 2005; Elman, 2000; Lee, W., 1996; Lee, H., 2000). In other words, Chinese traditional educational ideals and expectations attach both instrumental (pragmatic) and intrinsic (cultural) values to education. In contrast with these cultural ideals, in the past the public often adopted a pragmatic approach to education and consistently expected to acquire academic and literacy skills as well as achieve upward social mobility and personal development through education (Thøgersen, 2002). In particular, it was essential for people to achieve social mobility, gain financial returns or maintain their 'elite' status in communities through educational efforts, the culmination being to achieve success in imperial civil service exams (Miyazaki, 1976; Schulte, 2003). Although the civil service exams and traditional education officially ended at the beginning of the 1900s, their influence remains strong in spite of the social, cultural and political changes over the last century on the Chinese mainland (Thøgersen, 2002). Such traditional discourses have been transformed but reconstituted in the contemporary social, cultural and educational context on the Chinese mainland.

As China is one of the most densely populated countries in the world, academic competition has always been intense and this is particularly true of the past 10 years, largely due to the rapid expansion of tertiary education and the commercialization of education. The expansion in the tertiary educational sector, which should have alleviated the intensity of academic competition for higher education places among the public, has created new tensions as an increasing number of tertiary graduates remain unemployed after graduation (Bai, 2006; Hu, J., 2004; Postiglione, 2005). The high unemployment among tertiary graduates frustrates the traditional pursuit of social mobility and financial returns through education and sends shock waves through different levels of education, leading to greater competition for better grades and educational opportunities among teachers, parents and students (Phelps, 2005). The commercialization process, which has resulted in parents and students committing more and more financial resources to education under the newly introduced user-pay principle, has also added to the public's anxiety and stress. It has become widely recognized that only graduates from top universities will find it relatively easy to obtain employment. This has undoubtedly reinforced the hierarchical ranking of educational institutions and the critical importance of exam success at different levels (Bai, 2006; Hu, J., 2004; Zhao & Guo, 2002).

Learning of English on the Chinese Mainland

In order to succeed in such a competitive educational context, many Chinese started attaching great importance to the learning of foreign languages, especially English, and began to pursue academic studies abroad, most often in English-medium universities, as their courses are considered to be of higher value.

Since the late 1970s, the English language has become one of the most important means to reconnect China to the world and is promoted as a resource for economic prosperity in the face of globalization and the rise of the knowledge economy. Hence, recent educational reforms have been characterized by a greater role for English language learning (Bolton, 2002; He, 2005; Hu, G., 2002a, 2002b, 2003, 2005; Hu, X., 2004, 2005; Jiang, 2003; Ross, 1993; Zhao & Campbell, 1995; Yang, 2002). English forms part of the curriculum in almost every institution at all educational levels and success in English examinations is a prerequisite for advancement to higher levels of the system, especially for entry into the more prestigious universities. Various versions of the national secondary school English curriculum have consistently expressed a pragmatic and utilitarian view of English, echoing the century-long slogan for a self-strengthened China, stressing the instrumental value of the English language to individual students and the country (Adamson, 1998, 2002; Hu, G., 2002a, 2002b, 2003, 2005; Ng & Tang, 1997; Ross, 1993).

Critics may have regarded the unprecedented spread of English in the world as linguistic imperialism, the aim of which is to impose dominant social and cultural values on learners in different contexts (Pennycook, 1994; Phillipson, 1993). However, in the case of the Chinese mainland, public enthusiasm for learning English has also resulted from a genuine search for a competitive edge to enable individual learners to realize the traditional values attached to education in a highly competitive educational process (Nunan, 2003). 'Elite' families, like their predecessors in history, send their children to private schools or employ private tutors so that they can get an early start in the race to learn English. Better education and English competence are widely conceived by these emerging Chinese middle-class families as essential to securing a better future for their children. In fact, such expectations do not contradict the social functions of education promoted by the traditional educational discourses.

Research on Chinese students' English language learning motivation (Gao *et al.*, 2004, 2007) has identified the profound mediation of context on their motivation and found that Chinese students have strong *instrumental* and *cultural* motivation for learning English. In Gao *et al.*'s terms, instrumental motivation refers to learners' employment of the language as an information medium, for immediate achievement, individual development, going abroad (if for better personal development) or fulfilling social responsibilities. Cultural motivation refers to learners' learning a language out of interest (i.e. intrinsic motives), a desire to go abroad (for cultural experiences) or a sense of social obligation (learning English because of family expectations). In many senses, the concept of 'investment' (Norton Peirce, 1995) may be a better term to be used in exploring Chinese students' motives in learning English than the construct of motivation. In the light of the societal and traditional learning discourses, Chinese students are likely to put great efforts into learning English on the understanding 'that they will acquire a wider range of symbolic and material resources' (Norton Peirce, 1995: 17).

As an offshoot of this phenomenal interest in learning English, China has been witnessing a massive outflow of Chinese students to overseas institutions, in particular, to Anglophone countries where education is delivered through the medium of English (Gao, 2006a, 2008b; Gu & Brooks, 2008; Li & Bray, 2007; Tan & Simpson, 2008). In 2006, approximately 0.7 million Chinese students and scholars were involved in overseas academic studies and academic exchanges, most at English-medium universities (Jiaoyu Shewai Jianguang Xinxi Wang, 2006). It is in the context of this ongoing outflow of students from the Chinese mainland in search of better academic credentials and English competence that Hong Kong has become a favoured destination (Li, 2006; Li & Bray, 2007; Ming Pao, 2006a, 2006b; Yu, 2004).

Mainland Chinese Students in Hong Kong

As described in the previous sections, the rising number of mainland Chinese students moving to study in English-medium universities worldwide, including Hong Kong, is related to a strong belief in the role that education plays in one's social advancement, an increasingly competitive educational context and the prominent role of English on the Chinese mainland. The first officially sponsored group of mainland Chinese undergraduates arrived at Hong Kong's tertiary campuses 10 years ago. In 1999, the University Grants Committee (Hong Kong) and the Hong Kong Jockey Club started financing high school graduates with excellent academic records to pursue their first degrees in Hong Kong. To ensure the academic excellence of the scholarship recipients, these students were recruited from four top universities on the Chinese mainland, namely Peking University, Tsinghua University, Nanjing University and Fudan University.

From 2002, the Hong Kong Special Administrative Region (HKSAR) and the Chinese mainland governments introduced a scheme allowing self-financing mainland Chinese undergraduates to undertake study at Hong Kong's tertiary institutions. In 2003, under the Close Economic Partnership Agreement, procedures for mainland undergraduates to travel to Hong Kong were further simplified. Meanwhile, fee-paying schemes have expanded the enrolment of mainland undergraduates to include more provinces and cities, apart from Beijing, Shanghai and Nanjing. In 2006, 10,230 applicants reportedly applied for 270 undergraduate places allocated to mainland Chinese applicants by the university in the inquiry (Ming Pao, 2006a, 2006b). The tuition for these applicants has also been increasing steadily each year, ranging from 60,000 HKD (7500 USD) in 2004 to 100,000 HKD (12,500 USD) in 2007 for those who studied at that university.

As Hong Kong has a three-year university system in contrast to the four-year degree system on the Chinese mainland, the university referred to arranges for all the admitted candidates to spend their first year at one of the top universities on the Chinese mainland. Other universities in Hong Kong normally assign mainland undergraduates to some preparatory courses in Hong Kong. Mainland Chinese students often refer to preparatory studies on the Chinese mainland or in Hong Kong as 'Year 0' studies. This practice will change when Hong Kong adopts a four-year university system in 2012 as there will be no need for mainland Chinese students to undertake a year's preparatory studies.

To sum up, the rising number of applicants to Hong Kong tertiary institutions demonstrates the popularity of Hong Kong as a place for mainland Chinese parents to send their children for academic studies. It also suggests that the participants in the study, mostly fee-paying students at the university, are a highly select group of mainland Chinese students, who were born and grew up in more privileged family conditions than many other mainland Chinese students.

Challenges for mainland Chinese students in Hong Kong

Hong Kong, once a British colony, is often seen as an in-between place where East meets West. The majority of Hong Kong's population is Chinese, wrongly creating the impression that mainland Chinese students, also being Chinese, should have no cross-cultural and linguistic problems. However, although sharing the same ethnicity with their local counterparts, most mainland Chinese still have to face two daunting challenges, one linguistic, the other sociocultural, in their pursuit of English competence and educational excellence in Hong Kong.

Firstly, Hong Kong is characterized by a complex linguistic situation, which has been extensively studied (Benson, 1997; Boyle, 1997; Bolton & Lim, 2000; Evans, 2000; Gao *et al.*, 2000; Keung, 2006; Lai, 2001; Morrison & Lui, 2000; So, 1998). Cantonese is the dominant language in daily life and the favoured language for most social, cultural and political occasions, even though Hong Kong was until recently a British colony and English is one of its official languages. Meanwhile, the English language is widely used in the business and professional sectors and is constantly promoted as an important asset for individuals' career and social development as well as a crucial means for Hong Kong to retain its international standing. The status of Putonghua (often known as Mandarin Chinese), the national language variety shared by millions on the Chinese mainland, has been undergoing changes since the handover in 1997. Especially in recent years, when mainland Chinese travellers have become more visible in Hong Kong and have been contributing to Hong Kong's reviving economy, the local community has started attaching greater importance to Putonghua (Davison & Lai, 2007; Keung, 2006). However, although the number of Hong Kong residents claiming use of Putonghua has been rising steadily (Davison & Lai, 2007; Gao *et al.*, 2000; Keung, 2006), Cantonese remains and will most likely continue to remain for quite a long time, the major medium for socialization, while most mainland Chinese do not speak it.

Secondly, apart from the linguistic barrier, mainland Chinese and Hong Kong Chinese have had dramatically different social, cultural, historical and political experiences since Hong Kong was ceded to the British in the 19th century. For instance, when the Chinese mainland was still in a state of political turmoil, Hong Kong had already achieved enviable economic success in the region. These differences constitute a significant cultural gap differentiating the two Chinese groups despite the fact that they share the same ethnicity and a similar cultural heritage, problematizing any homogeneous view of Chinese learners (Flowerdew *et al.*, 2002; Ho *et al.*, 2003; Li *et al.*, 1995; Ma & Fung, 1999; Schack & Schack, 2005). As strange 'siblings' to local students, mainland Chinese students may have to face the vestiges of an 'othering' process, in which mainland Chinese were often portrayed as uncivilized and unsophisticated in contrast to the modern cosmopolitan Hong Kong people. Such perceptions are largely based on differences in the two groups' experiences in different arenas of daily life, which are likely to create negative social attitudes on both sides (Fung, 2001; Ho *et al.*, 2003; Li *et al.*, 1995; Ma & Fung, 1999; Schack & Schack, 2005). In recent years, although the differences between mainland Chinese and local Chinese in Hong Kong are diminishing, it is fair to say that these differences still constitute sociocultural barriers between two groups of people sharing the same ethnic origin (Gao *et al.*, 2000; Ho *et al.*, 2003). The persisting 'us–them' differences may create potential problems in the socialization process for mainland Chinese students in Hong Kong.

Institutional settings: Campus and hall life

The university considered in this study is one of the leading English-medium universities in the region and English is assumed to be the sole medium of instruction and avenue for pursuing academic studies. The university is also one of the most internationalized universities in Hong Kong, having a high percentage of non-local faculty members and students, thus facilitating the use of English on campus. Nevertheless, as confirmed by my observations, Cantonese remains the dominant language on campus, in student halls, student group discussions and social functions. This creates a difficult situation for the participants in the academic learning process: the dominant medium of socialization (Cantonese) differs from the expected medium of instruction (English) while most mainland Chinese students do not speak Cantonese and want to improve their English.

Campus and student halls are the physical settings for the communities of practice where mainland Chinese students experience university education and language learning. Like many other non-local students, most mainland Chinese students live in the university-administered student halls, which are subsidized by the University Grants Committee (Hong Kong). Most of the university's halls have strong traditions of education and distinctive cultures, which are recognized as part of the broad experiential education provided by the university. The halls are proud of their education schemes, with their variety of social, cultural and sports activities, aiming to bring all hall residents together for unique experiences of collective life (HKU Post, 2006). However, most of these hall functions use Cantonese as the medium of communication and are largely built on the respective halls' own traditions, while incoming non-local students have distinctly different linguistic backgrounds and prior sociocultural experiences. Hence, mainland Chinese students, as well as other non-local students, are often both linguistically and socioculturally excluded or at least marginalized in relation to these functions.

Although many mainland Chinese students are active in residential halls, in the local students' debates and meetings that I have witnessed, non-local students, especially mainland Chinese students, were often a cause of concern. They were seen as a potential threat to the hall cultural traditions as they are more likely to be non-participatory members in the collective life. Many mainland Chinese students are more inclined to focus their time and energy on academic accomplishments rather than on other social and cultural contributions to local student groups. This does not mean that mainland students in Hong Kong are the only students who are willing to sacrifice their social lives for academic pursuits. Rather, they are being pragmatic by setting different priorities from those pursued by local students in daily life since they do not have the luxury of ease enjoyed by local students in their own home setting and are driven by an urgency to secure and maximize their educational investment. According to the Immigration Ordinance, as non-local residents, to obtain a position in Hong Kong, they have to demonstrate that they are more employable than local graduates. To receive further education in Hong Kong and abroad, they need to show their academic prowess in the form of a high grade-point-average (GPA). Good academic results are also needed to justify the heavy financial investment in education by their families.

As the number of non-local, in particular mainland Chinese, students increases in halls, they take up more and more places once reserved for local students. Local students, who fear that their hall traditions might be undermined by the diminishing presence of local students, even held demonstrations against the allocation of non-local students to the UGC-funded residences (HKU Post, 2006). In one of the emails circulating about the demonstration, the policy of giving priority to non-local students in residential place allocation was cited as a waste of taxpayers' money. However, in spite of such unpleasant incidents, the relationship between non-local and local students in general remains amicable and friendly. It seems that only on particular occasions, some one-off remarks are made or incidents flare up, reminding both sides, in particular mainland Chinese students, that they are somehow outsiders. However, such occasional but often emotionally intense incidents are indicative of contextual constraints, mediating mainland students' strategic language learning. It leads to the question as to whether or not mainland Chinese students can improve their English through their socialization with local students.

Conclusion

In this chapter, I have explained why mainland Chinese students migrate to English-medium universities and depicted in detail the learning context and institutional setting in Hong Kong. The picture reveals many important contextual elements relevant to these mainland students' pursuit of English competence in this particular institutional setting. To start with, it presents a highly fluid and dynamic language learning environment where the relationships among three high-profile languages (English, Cantonese and Putonghua) are shifting. The portrayal also highlights the existing linguistic and cultural gaps between mainland Chinese people and the majority of the local Chinese population; these gaps are indicative of a somewhat uneasy social relationship between the two. The inconsistency between English as the medium of academic instruction and Cantonese as the medium of socialization in the university is also likely to present itself as another challenge for the newly arrived mainland Chinese students. It was within these contextual conditions that the inquiry into the mediation of changing contexts on the participants' strategy use aimed to reveal insights about the interaction between context and agency underlying their strategy use. The following chapters will explore to what extent the participants' prior learning experiences on the Chinese mainland might have influenced their adoption of strategies for learning English and how contextual conditions mediated their strategic learning efforts in Hong Kong. Chapters 4 and 5 report findings from studies conducted in the first and third research phases, thus providing a general picture of the participants' strategy use as a group on the Chinese mainland and in Hong Kong. The second follow-up study (Phase 2), capturing the process of change in the case study participants' strategy use, is reported in Chapter 6.

Chapter 4
On the Chinese Mainland

Chapter 3 has established the broad contextual conditions for the participants' language learning on the Chinese mainland and in Hong Kong. This chapter now reports on findings from the study in Phase 1, in which newly arrived mainland Chinese undergraduates were interviewed in August and September 2004 about their experiences of learning English and their strategy use on the Chinese mainland. This helped establish a baseline for comparison when the same participants were interviewed again about their language learning experiences in Hong Kong (see Chapter 5).

Study in Phase 1 (August–September 2004)

The primary aim in the first research phase was to capture the developmental process of the research participants' strategy use through interpreting their learning experiences on the Chinese mainland. It aimed to answer the following research questions:

(1) What were the distinctive features of the participants' strategy use on the Chinese mainland?
(2) How did these participants come to adopt particular patterns of strategy use as displayed in their interview accounts?

With the insights from my previous research (Gao, 2003, 2006a) and the adoption of the sociocultural perspective outlined in Chapter 2 (Figure 2.5), I also found it necessary to include the following research questions in Phase 1:

(1) How did the participants construct their language learning discursively in terms of motivation (motives or values) and beliefs on the Chinese mainland?

(2) How did social agents mediate their strategy use?
(3) What were the roles of cultural artefacts in their development of particular learning strategies?

In this phase, 22 arriving mainland Chinese undergraduates, who
attended a non-compulsory summer English course at the university, vol-
unteered for the study and were interviewed, using a semi-structured
interview guide (Appendix 1). Fifteen of them were interviewed again in
the third phase about their language learning experiences in Hong Kong
approximately 20 months later (Table 4.1). As can be seen in Table 4.1,
most of them were studying courses like business as these courses were
highly popular among mainland Chinese applicants. Most of these participants were from large cities like Beijing and from cities in southeast
China. Participants from Beijing had generally grown up in a monolingual
setting speaking as their mother tongue the dialect forming the phonetic
base of Putonghua, whereas other participants spoke various dialects in
addition to Putonghua. Only one participant in the study (Yaojing) spoke
Cantonese. Another noticeable feature associated with the study participants was that female participants outnumbered males. Research in other
contexts suggests that female learners seem to be more motivated to learn
languages than males (e.g. Pritchard & Maki, 2006). Consequently, it is
probably not surprising that more female mainland Chinese students
decided to take this non-compulsory English course.

Each interview normally lasted for an hour. The interviews were conducted in Putonghua (Chinese) except for one participant (Yaojing) who
opted for English (see Table 4.1). All the interviews were audio recorded
and transcribed verbatim, except for one recording, which was not
included due to the extremely poor sound quality. For data analysis, a
'paradigmatic approach' (Erickson, 2004; Smeyers & Verhesschen, 2001)
was adopted in interpreting the biographical narratives produced by the
study participants, which involved both a deductive and an inductive
analytical procedure. The first step was to go through the biographical
data to obtain a global understanding of each individual participant's
previous English learning experiences with a focus on their strategy use
on the Chinese mainland. Then, informed by the research questions and
interpretative framework (Figure 2.5), I derived a set of preliminary
coding categories, including strategy use, discourses about language
learning, influential social agents and artefacts (materials), and used
constant questioning and comparing steps to search for the participants'
references to these preliminary coding categories (Patton, 1990; Strauss &
Corbin, 1998).

Table 4.1 List of the participants in the 1st and 3rd phases

No.	Name	Gender	Place of origin	Faculty	1st phase	3rd phase	NB
1	Rachel*	F	Fujian	Business	Yes	Yes	1st interview in Chinese, 2nd in English
2	Luonan	F	Fujian	Business	Yes	Yes	Both interviews in Chinese
3	Jingwei *	F	Fujian	Business	Yes	Yes	Both interviews in Chinese
4	Mengshi*	M	Zhejiang	Business	Yes	Yes	1st interview in Chinese, 2nd interview in English
5	Moya	F	Beijing	Business	Yes	No	Interview in Chinese
6	Floyd	M	Fujian	Business	Yes	No	Interview in Chinese
7	Jeffreys	M	Fujian	Science	Yes	No	Interview in Chinese
8	Yuran	M	Jiangsu	Science	Yes	Yes	Both interviews in Chinese
9	Yuka	F	Beijing	Business	Yes	Yes	1st interview not transcribed due to technical error, 2nd interview in Chinese
10	Ran Ran	F	Beijing	Law	Yes	No	Interview in Chinese

11	Tian Zhou	M	Beijing	Business	Yes	Yes	Both interviews in Chinese
12	Dongxu	F	Jiangsu	Business	Yes	Yes	Both interviews in Chinese
13	Liu*	F	Fujian	Business	Yes	Yes	1st interview in Chinese, 2nd interview in English
14	Jeff	M	Zhejiang	Science	Yes	Yes	Both interviews in Chinese
15	Jessy	F	Beijing	Business	Yes	No	Interview in Chinese
16	Yaojing	F	Guangdong	Science	Yes	Yes	Both interviews in English
17	Yu*	F	Fujian	Architecture	Yes	Yes	Both interviews in Chinese
18	Ting	F	Beijing	Business	Yes	No	Interview in Chinese
19	Meng	F	Beijing	Science	Yes	Yes	Both interviews in Chinese
20	Zhixuan*	M	Beijing	Science	Yes	Yes	Both interviews in Chinese
21	Cheng	F	Fujian	Business	Yes	No	Interview in Chinese
22	Jing	F	Fujian	Law	Yes	Yes	Both interviews in Chinese

Participants with '*' were involved in the longitudinal follow-up study (Phase 2)
All the participants' names are pseudonyms

In the following sections, I will present findings on particular patterns of strategy use identified from the interview data through analysis. The rest of this chapter demonstrates how the participants came to adopt particular patterns of strategies. Particular attention is paid to the data revealing how societal learning discourses, various social agents and artefacts mediated their efforts to learn English. The interview extracts that appear in the following sections are all translations from Chinese except for those noted otherwise.

Participants' Strategy Use on the Chinese Mainland

As the participants were required to spend one year in leading mainland Chinese universities before commencing their studies in Hong Kong, two stages of learning English on the Chinese mainland could be identified in the data. The first stage relates to their learning of English in school settings, where exam-oriented teaching and learning were the most pronounced theme. The second is their preparatory year in mainland Chinese universities prior to their arrival in Hong Kong. During that year, many exam-oriented learning features disappeared from their strategy use and most participants were active in preparing themselves linguistically for English-medium instruction at the university.

In the data analysis process, I went through all references to their engagement in acquiring English competence and coded them as their strategy use in learning English. For instance, in the following two interview extracts, Jessy and Jeff described how they learnt English on the Chinese mainland:

> When I was taking the TOEFL course, I also tried to memorize some words. […] There was a book full of word lists. I looked at five words at one time and then closed the book. I tried to recall them. Then I looked at the next five words. After going through one page, I looked at the words on the page in reverse order. I liked to look at a word a few more times rather than spend five minutes on one word because it was just boring to look at a word for such a long time. (Jessy, 1st interview)

> In the past, what I did most was memorize words. […] after looking at a word four or five times, I could remember it. (Jeff, 1st interview)

Jessy's quote was a reference to the use of a vocabulary memorization strategy employed when she talked about her language learning experiences during her preparatory year. In the second interview extract, Jeff referred to the use of a vocabulary memorization strategy in his secondary school. Although both learners talked about using similar strategies, Jessy memorized words of her own accord for an examination that she chose to take during the preparatory year in a mainland Chinese university while Jeff felt obliged to memorize words for a compulsory English course at school. This background information enabled me to code the two extracts into different categories of strategy use ('obligatory' versus 'voluntary') in two different learning stages, secondary school and preparatory year. In addition, if particular participants made several references to the same strategy in the data, only one count was taken for each learning stage. It was from such a coding and counting process that findings presented in Table 4.2 emerged.

Describing strategy use in the interview data

While Table 4.2 gives an overview of the participants' strategy use on the Chinese mainland, the interview data bring more information about how they used these strategies. As recorded in Table 4.2, one of the most widespread strategies for the participants in learning English on the Chinese mainland was memorization, confirming the findings of previous research on Chinese learners, who have been seen as prone to using memorization strategies (Fan, 2003; Gu, 2003; Kember, 2000; Kennedy, 2002; Watkins, 2000; Watkins & Biggs, 1996). All the participants repeatedly referred to memorizing words as a major part of their English learning experiences like Jessy and Jeff in their interview extracts. In spite of its popularity, the data suggest that most participants did not really enjoy memorizing words. The following extract is indicative of the problems that participants might have with memorization:

> My father forced me to memorize words in the beginning. [...] When I was still in primary school, I had memorized vocabulary for Year 2 university students. However, if you test me on what a particular word means, I do not actually remember it. I just know that I have seen this word before. I only had some vague impression of it. (Yu, 1st interview)

The above quote reveals that Yu considered it an unpleasant task to spend time memorizing words. She admitted that she was often 'forced' to do so because of her parents. Later on, as she reflected on the effectiveness of memorization, she also found that her memorization efforts did not help her to achieve long-term retention of words and consequently felt that it was futile to have put so much effort into memorizing. Therefore, it was

Table 4.2 Strategies reported by the participants ($N = 21$)

Strategy types	Strategy items	Counts	
		Schools	Pre-HK
English as an academic course and exam-related (obligatory)	Do course readings and exam-related reading materials	15	–
	Memorize words	20	–
	Follow teachers' teaching	17	2
	Work on simulation exam papers/ exercise books	21	–
	Memorize and recite texts	12	–
	Practise writing	7	–
	Listening to cassettes	7	–
Voluntary (with little external coercion but more external encouragement)	Receive extra English tuition	12	8
	Watch English TV/movies/play English PC games	11	11
	Listen to radio/recordings /songs/ other materials	6	5
	Read English magazines or newspaper or materials	4	9
	Surf English websites	1	3
	Use software to learn English	1	7
	Memorize words	2	8
	Memorize English texts/lyrics/ sentences	1	2
	Practise English with others/ participate in English corners	3	7
	Write English diaries/blogs	2	2
	Murmur to myself	1	–
	Participate in English-related competitions	1	1

(Continued)

Table 4.2 *Continued*

Strategy types	Strategy items	Counts Schools	Pre-HK
Others (specific strategies in the learning process)	Pay attention to language used during listening and reading	8	7
	Retain the memory of words/texts in contexts (listening or reading)	3	5
	Guess meaning from contexts	3	1
	Rote memory (look at a word several times)	4	3
	Involve others (teachers, parents and/or peers) in learning English	13	7
	Look up new words in dictionaries (paper or electronic)	3	5
	Write down a new word in a note book	–	1
	Limit the use of Chinese in learning English	1	3
	Imitate others in speaking English	1	–

not surprising to see that participants like Yu had feelings of aversion towards memorization and made less effort to memorize after exam pressure was lifted at the end of their secondary education (as displayed in Table 4.2). Some participants like Liu even claimed that they hated memorizing:

> I would not take a vocabulary list and try to memorize it. I hated it so much. (Liu, 1st interview)

Apart from memorizing words, the participants mentioned in the interviews about memorizing grammar rules, textbook texts, English essays, speeches and song lyrics (see Table 4.2). While 12 participants memorized textbooks for classroom recitation and grammar points for examination, one participant also mentioned selecting famous English essays, speeches or lyrics for voluntary memorization at different stages of learning. As indicated in Table 4.2, these memorization efforts were largely abandoned after they left secondary school. However, a few participants found them useful because they helped them to internalize different ways of expressing themselves and gave them a feel of the English language. Zhixuan commented on his memorization efforts in the following extract:

> I reflected on the fact that I had recited so many English texts. I think that it helps improve my linguistic skills when reading these texts aloud for memorization. For instance, I could improve my intonation … I think that it is important to recite. Recitation is important when learning a language. I recited when learning my mother tongue. (Zhixuan, 1st interview)

Two participants mentioned that they memorized lyrics and classical English essays during the transition year on the Chinese mainland and even after they arrived in Hong Kong. Jing recalled his experience:

> I have tried to memorize song lyrics. They were actually quite simple, but they helped me to express deep feelings. […] I learnt to express the same thing in many different ways. (Jing, 1st interview)

According to the interview data, other highly popular strategies among the participants included taking extracurricular courses and employing private English tutors. Both actions seem to have had similar functions: they extended the participants' exposure to the English language and hence their learning time. These strategic moves often gave participants some opportunities to learn what they could not learn in school settings and thus gave them a competitive edge. In the data (Table 4.2), eight participants attended various courses for international English proficiency tests during the preparatory year. In the interviews, it was one of the participants (Ran Ran) who referred to the act of taking an extra course as a strategy to improve her linguistic competence and examination performance:

Gao: Could you tell me how you learnt English?
Ran Ran: I did not try to learn English. I mean that I have never
              thought of taking a special course to learn English.
              (Ran Ran, 1st interview)

Ran Ran, who denied investing such intentional effort in learning English in the extract above, admitted in the later part of the interview that she had taken an IELTS preparation course when she was preparing for the IELTS test in senior secondary school. Another learner (Meng) observed that her classmates took extracurricular English courses either because they were pursuing learning objectives other than the school's teaching objectives or because school teachers failed to satisfy their needs in learning English:

> I had a few good friends, whose families put great emphasis on learning English. They started learning when they were very young because they were preparing themselves for studying abroad. [...] they started taking courses outside of school hours when they were very young. [...] So we had different English levels. People like me would follow our teachers' teaching. Others learnt more outside. Maybe in some good schools, teachers would tell you how much you need to learn or read. [...] In general, I think that we learnt more English outside. (Meng, 1st interview)

The popularity of having additional English exposure may depend on individual participants' preferences as well as their families' financial circumstances. The participants' privileged financial conditions enabled them to gain access to more quality language input and exposure, which helped distinguish them from other students in terms of learning achievement. However, there was one strategy, which also expanded the participants' exposure to English in a peculiar way and which seems to have equalized the participants' learning opportunities with those of other students. In schools, they were required to spend a lot of time working on simulation examination papers in preparation for high-stakes compulsory examinations. All participants knew that it was crucial for them to have good examination results as examinations decided whether or not they would be able to have further educational opportunities beyond their current level of schooling. As these compulsory examinations disappeared after they completed their secondary education, the use of this strategy virtually ceased among all the participants (see Table 4.2). When talking about their English language learning experiences at senior high school, Luonan described their classroom English language learning in a way that was not uncommon among the participants:

> At that time, we had exercise questions and mock papers. Every day, we copied words. Every week, we had dictation exercises. Then we had one mock exam after another. (Luonan, 1st interview)

Although they felt that this strategy might have helped them to achieve good examination scores, most were quite critical about learning English for the sake of taking examinations. Such an approach to learning English might have made English language learning boring for the participants. Dongxu complained:

> I often just focused on grammar points for the sake of answering an exam question properly. I seldom had opportunities to use these grammar points in daily life. [...] I did a lot of simulation exam exercises, such as cloze, reading comprehension and so on. I did not feel that I improved my English competence. (Dongxu, 1st interview)

The data suggest that the participants had many strategies in common in learning English on the Chinese mainland, but there were also individual elements in their displayed strategy use. Many participants had developed a unique set of strategies to enhance their English language learning. For instance, some of them enjoyed listening to the English radio and to songs (e.g. Ran Ran and Liu). Others liked watching TV and movies (e.g. Mengshi and Yu). Some participants even tried to join English competitions to motivate themselves to learn more English (e.g. Ran Ran). Others would also try to talk to English speakers, both native and non-native in English (e.g. Moya, Jeffreys, Liu and Jing). The participants tried to read widely, in most cases because they were encouraged or instructed by their teachers to do so (e.g. Tianzhou and Meng), but in a few other cases, because they did have a strong desire to learn more English than the teachers could teach them (e.g. Yaojing). As recorded in Table 4.2, the number of participants using these alternative strategies increased when the participants were released from the intensive preparation for the National College Entrance Examination. The prospect of undertaking Hong Kong tertiary studies through the medium of English had also been an incentive for some participants to put more effort into learning English during their transitory year in mainland Chinese institutions as they wanted to achieve an appropriate command of English to cope with the English-medium tertiary instruction ahead in Hong Kong. While some transitory institutions in Beijing provided opportunities for the participants to receive special English tuition, students in other institutions, in particular in Fujian province, arranged to employ English tutors at their own expense to prepare for their arrival in Hong Kong (e.g. Rachel, Luonan, Jingwei and Yu).

In short, the participants in this study revealed in the biographical interviews that, prior to coming to Hong Kong, they had used memorization strategies extensively to memorize words, texts and grammar points to achieve exam-related success. They had also attempted to increase their exposure to English, often in the form of intensive exam preparation activities including working on simulation examination papers and taking extra English courses. As the exam pressure declined at the end of their secondary education, motivated participants started focusing more on improving linguistic competence and used more strategies to extend their exposure to English and increase their practice opportunities through a variety of activities, including listening to English songs, watching English movies and reading English books. With such strategy shifts in motion prior to their arrival in Hong Kong, it seems important to explore the mechanism underlying the participants' strategy use as documented in Table 4.2. The rest of this chapter does this by examining how the participants' strategy use was related to a process mediated by popular discourses, social agents, as well as artefacts and the practices associated with these artefacts, in accordance with the interpretative framework outlined in Chapter 2 (Figure 2.5).

Discourses about Learning English

As learning strategies are often seen as goal-oriented, intentionally invoked and effortful learning behaviour in LLS research (Dörnyei, 2005; Tseng *et al.*, 2006; Yang, 1999), this inquiry recognizes that the participants' motivational and belief discourses could reveal the processes underlying their strategy use. In the interviews, although varying in tone and expression, they gave answers of similar effect to the view that 'the English language is a tool' (Yaojing, English original), when asked to describe why they learnt English.

Although the quotation emphasizes the instrumental value of the language, further analysis of the data drew on Gao *et al.*'s (2004, 2007) study on motivation types among Chinese students and revealed that their discourses about learning English were indicative of a mixture of instrumental and cultural motivational discourses (Table 4.3). This section demonstrates that their discourses about learning English echo the popular societal and traditional discourses about learning, stressing the instrumental value of learning and education (Bai, 2005; Elman, 2000; Lee, W., 1996; Lee, H., 2000; Miyazaki, 1976; Thøgersen, 2002). It shows that most participants were encouraged and, in many cases, obliged to absorb the societal and traditional discourses about learning by various social agents and their use of cultural artefacts, which had led to their use of strategies that they were

Table 4.3 The participants' motivational discourses (*N* = 21)

No.	Participants expressing motivational discourses	Numbers
1	Culturally oriented motivational discourses	8
2	Instrumentally oriented motivational discourses	21

critical of. For instance, they did not believe that they should learn for examinations but nevertheless they did so because of the perceived contextual reality and mediation from social agents like teachers.

Instrumental motivational discourses

The most popular motives given by the participants may include, though are not necessarily limited to, the following statements, echoing a shared perception of English as an important academic subject and a stepping stone to further studies in the world:

> The English language was an academic subject. (Jeff, 1st interview)

> Why did I learn English? In the beginning, it was for the sake of the exam. (Meng, 1st interview)

> The English language is a tool for teaching, learning and communication. I had to learn it. (Dongxu, 1st interview)

The beliefs thus expressed of these participants indicate that their adoption was related to their educational experiences on the Chinese mainland. For instance, both Jeff's and Meng's schooling experiences had reinforced a strong belief that English was a crucial academic subject for them to learn and master. Dongxu highlighted the fact that many participants like her 'had to' learn English. All the participants were also aware of the fact that good English examination results decided whether or not they would have access to further educational opportunities abroad.

Beyond the confines of the school setting, the participants sensed the critical importance of English in their lives. Cheng and Luonan indicate that they believed that an appropriate level of English was important for employment:

> Because everybody else was learning English, I had to learn English, too. [...] you would have to take English examinations if you wanted to do anything, for instance, look for jobs. I had to learn English. (Cheng, 1st interview)

> If you cannot pass the College English Test band 4 and 6, you cannot find jobs. (Luonan, 1st interview)

As employment was an important justification for the participants' educational efforts in traditional educational discourses (Thøgersen, 2002), they did not see that they had any other option than to learn English. If they had thought otherwise, they would not have become participants in this inquiry. To some extent, these quotes shed more light on the external societal mediation on the values and attitudes that the participants attached to the learning of English. In particular, among all the justifications that the participants gave in the interview, one interview extract particularly deserves attention. Ting's statement displays her awareness of the complicated local and global processes which had made it essential for her to learn English. There is a provocative quality about her answer as if the question why she learnt English itself did not seem to make any sense to her:

> It was a 'tianjingdiyi' (天经地义, undoubtedly, there should be no question about it) thing for me. [...] Nobody asked me why I had to learn Chinese. [...] when I was young, I was told that we need to learn English. Then the globalization process came. It made me feel that the whole world needed to speak English. Therefore, it was very natural for me to learn English. (Ting, 1st interview)

In her discourses, English was no longer a foreign language to be learned but something that had to be acquired, like her own mother tongue. This can well be related to the fact that English is currently being promoted on the Chinese mainland not as a foreign language but as an essential skill (Jiang, 2003; Tsui, 2004). However, this does not seem to reduce the instrumental value of English in her perception.

In conclusion, the interview data reveal that the participants' learning discourses emphatically stress the centrality of English proficiency, often in terms of high-stakes examination performance and its relation to social mobility. Their discourses reflect the social attitudes towards the learning of English and values attached to the English language on the Chinese mainland. English has been promoted in China as an important means for the country to reconnect itself to the world for better access to technology and business opportunities (Jiang, 2003; Ross, 1993; Zhao & Campbell, 1995). In other words, the participants were probably exposed to societal and traditional discourses about learning as they grew up and had more or less internalized these discourses, which in turn became a powerful inner drive motivating their strategy use. As shown in the coming sections, their exposure to external learning discourses was mediated by agents like parents and teachers. However, in spite of the mediation of such instrumental discourses, the interview data suggest that a few participants, though clearly in minority, did adhere to the intrinsic values of English.

Cultural motivational discourses

Although the instrumental discourses about learning English were a dominant theme in the interview data, eight participants expressed cultural motivation for learning English (Table 4.3). In many cases, such cultural discourses were often integrated with the overall instrumental discourses. However, some of the participants were straightforward about their cultural learning motives. For instance, Jessy and Jing regarded English as a means to appreciate works originally published in the English language as well as the cultures of various English-speaking countries. Such participants often turned out to be those who had ambitions of pursuing academic studies in English-medium universities abroad:

> I can also read works in their originals. Translated works are different from their originals. (Jessy, 1st interview)

> I was deeply interested in English. [...] At that time, I was also interested in Western culture, American culture. I looked forward to going abroad (Jing, 1st interview)

Participants like Ran Ran enjoyed experiencing cultural products in the English language. Her account of being a fan of English pop songs indicates her intrinsic interest in the language, an interest that might have been easily obliterated by the dominant instrumental discourses among many other participants. This cultural motivation did add a personal feature to her strategy use as she liked to use the strategy of listening to pop songs to learn English on the Chinese mainland:

> I was interested in English, interested in listening to English sounds. [...] I was just interested in listening to English radio programs. [...] I was interested in English because it could bring me pleasure. Although I had more pragmatic motives for learning English these days, this interest has by no means disappeared. (Ran Ran, 1st interview)

Moreover, a few of these participants saw that a good command of English was related to who they were in the past and who they would be in the future, in other words, their self-identities seen in terms of their constructed social relationship to others (Norton Peirce, 1995; Norton, 2000). Many quotes that appeared in previous sections also indicate such awareness. When Ting described the learning of English as 'tianjingdiyi' (天经地义), she also projected herself as one of the globally mobile citizens of the future. Other participants had more local concerns. They were concerned that English proficiency would enhance their social status in the student community in which they found themselves, in particular, among their peers. They were also highly motivated by good examination results to learn English since good examination results often provided them with a sense of satisfaction over their learning achievements.

Far more importantly, good examination results decided their ranking among their peers at school and subsequently the social status they could achieve through the educational path (Miyazaki, 1976). Seeing that they were the top students in their previous schools, it was hardly surprising that these participants were quite competition-minded since winning competitions was essential for them to maintain their 'elite' status or identity. This might have created a strong impetus forcing them to prove that they could excel in English and adopt various strategies for this purpose, as suggested in the following extracts:

> I liked to study English because I liked to have good exam results. (Jessy, 1st interview)

> I also participated in some English competitions and got some English certificates. I may have sounded a bit opportunistic for I talked about my competitions and awards. However, these awards made me a distinguished English learner. (Ran Ran, 1st interview)

> I learnt the English language because I had to use it. [...] If you can speak English well, others will consider you highly educated. You will have a higher social status. (Liu, 1st interview)

In short, the participants considered English a means to access its culture and cultural products. They also believed that their English proficiency might have helped them to negotiate their relationships with others and fulfill what they desired to be, a belief that seemed to have motivated their investment and strategy use in learning English. The participants' association of learning success with their identities was also cultural in the sense that it evoked the traditional utilitarian discourses about education, which emphasize social promotion and individual perfection through educational efforts (Elman, 2000; Lee, W., 1996; Lee, H., 2000; Miyazaki, 1976; Thøgersen, 2002).

Mediating Agents

The data in the previous section revealed that the participants' motives (values and attitudes) in learning English were closely linked to the societal and traditional expectations of learning and educational efforts (Lee, 2000; Thøgersen, 2002). They also relate their motivational discourses to their educational experiences, which exposed the participants to the widespread societal and traditional learning discourses. In many senses, the participants' motives or values and attitudes in learning English can be regarded as resulting from their internalization of the societal and traditional learning discourses. Sociocultural theorists argue that learning is a socialization process (Lantolf, 2000; Lave & Wenger, 1990; Parks & Raymond, 2004; Wenger, 1998), in which the roles of social agents, either supportive or restrictive, are critical in fostering particular sets of values, beliefs and practices among individual learners. The participants in the study were not born with their current beliefs and motives (values and attitudes) but acquired them as they grew up in their social groups. Therefore, it is necessary to examine their strategy use and motivational discourses along with the behaviour of various social agents who had mediated their learning experiences on the Chinese mainland.

Informed by my early study on Chinese learners (Gao, 2006a), three types of social agents were identified as having mediated their development as English language learners in the data interpretation process: the participants' family, English teachers and peers. The relevant data were sub-coded into their mediation on the participants' learning discourses, cultural artefacts, material conditions and strategy use. Firstly, the participants' families were found to be actively involved in the participants' English learning. Chinese parents, like other Asian parents, have been noted for their zealous involvement in their child's academic development (Bai, 2005; Lee, W., 1996; Lee, H., 2000). Secondly, in comparison with parents, English teachers were more likely to mediate the participants' learning English and strategy use because of their role in the learning process and authority associated with the Chinese cultural tradition (Cheng, 2000; Cortazzi & Jin, 1996; Kember, 2000; Stephens, 1997; Watkins, 2000; Wen & Clement, 2003). Thirdly, peer interaction was found to be important in shaping their attitudes towards English and heightening their awareness of particular ways of learning English. This section describes in detail how these social agents mediated participants' strategy use and other relevant aspects of language learning as identified in the inquiry.

Family influences

The data reveal that the participants' families were involved both directly and indirectly in their language learning and hence had an important role in mediating their development as English learners. The family, mostly the participants' parents, mediated their language learning in three ways as listed in Table 4.4.

Firstly, they influenced the participants' discourses about learning English by mediating societal and traditional learning discourses, motivating or propelling them to learn English. In some cases, they enhanced their learning motivation by reproducing target cultures or communities.

In others, they attempted to foster particular learning beliefs, which were used by the participants to guide and justify their strategy use. Secondly, they invested heavily in providing good learning conditions, creating learning opportunities and recruiting other agents, particularly teachers, to mediate the participants' learning of English. Thirdly, they personally offered assistance in the participants' learning process and it was found that they developed the participants to be effective language learners in terms of strategy use by coercion and nurturing.

At the discursive level

At least half of the participants mentioned that their families had exerted a profound influence on their learning attitudes and motivation. Members of the family often attempted to instil positive attitudes towards learning English among the participants from the moment they started learning English or even earlier, highlighting the critical importance of the language to the participants' future. The power of such discourse on young minds is captured in the following conversation between Luonan and me:

Luonan: I had already realized the enormous importance of the English language when I was three.
Gao: You were three?
Luonan: I am not exaggerating! It started from when I could remember things. I remembered that I was told by my grandfather-in-law, grandmother-in-law, grandfather, grandmother, father, mother, aunties and uncles. They all tried their best to convince me that English, as a language, is very important! (Luonan, 1st interview)

In addition, many participants apparently had relatives who had first-hand contact with target communities and cultures. Their familiarity with target communities and cultures gave them authority and prestige as role models, enhancing the participants' language learning motivation. They showed to the participants how much the English language could change their life and social status. For example, Zhixuan was inspired by American culture brought back by his uncle and aunt and this played a crucial role in changing his attitudes towards learning English, propelling him to use more strategies to improve his English:

Gao: Why are you so much influenced by the West (US)?
Zhixuan: My uncle and auntie have influenced me a lot. They have been to the States. They brought a lot of ... they are quite AMERICANIZED ..., many thoughts or ideas, which influenced me a lot. (Zhixuan, 1st interview)

In the case of Rachel, her father, who had been overseas, taught her English when she was young but also told her how important the English language was to him when he was abroad. In addition, her father encouraged her in the belief that she should learn to speak English before learning to write it:

> First of all, my father, from the very beginning, he has been telling me of the importance of English. He had been abroad himself, for a few years. He knows how important English is to us when abroad. (Rachel, 1st interview)

> My father, my father said that I should learn to speak first, then, well, just like kids. They all learn to speak first, then they learn to write. (Rachel, 1st interview)

Ting's father used to play English recordings while she was working on something else so that she could learn English at the same time. She did not question the utility of this, simply accepting her father's explanation:

Gao: How did you learn English then?
Ting: At that time, my father played *'English 900'* to me. I did not really understand it and just listened to it.
Gao: What a filial daughter!
Ting: Well, he would let me do what I was doing, for example, he would let me continue doing my own things. He played the cassette in the background and just told me to pay some attention to it. He said it was like the child, who was born and learnt Chinese while listening to others. The child did not understand everything, but he listened and learnt to speak Chinese! (Ting, 1st interview)

As a result of the parents' enthusiastic involvement, the participants were exposed to powerful discourses about learning English in multiple ways in their family settings and their discourses about learning English were strongly shaped by their close family (see Table 4.4). This finding helps explain why they appeared to have internalized a learning discourse that regards the English language not only as the means of gaining material goods but also the key to sociocultural capital required for their desired social status and identities (Jiang, 2003; Ross, 1993; Zhao & Campbell, 1995).

At the learning condition level

In at least 18 participants' narratives, parents were portrayed as active agents in providing learning conditions, facilitating their language learning and use of particular strategies. This observation seems to fit the well-known stereotypes of Chinese parents (Stevenson & Stigler, 1992).

Table 4.4 Participants who claimed that their family mediated their language learning ($N = 21$)

No.	Role	Mediation	Numbers
1	Language learning advocates	Learning discourses	11
2	Language learning facilitators	Learning conditions, materials and opportunities	18
3	Collaborators with teachers		13
4	Language learning advisors	Direct involvement in learning and strategy use	7
5	Learning coercers		2
6	Learning nurturers		4

Moreover, most participants were from well-off, professional and middle-class urban families. Consequently, their parents could afford to invest heavily in their child's academic studies. They typically arranged good language learning environments for the participants, such as installing satellite TV channels to provide quality English TV programmes, employing native speakers as home tutors, purchasing English movies or English magazines and choosing the right schools. They would even create learning opportunities for the participants to practise using particular strategies. For example, Moya was encouraged by her English-speaking father, who had studied overseas, to practise speaking English at home:

> At that time, my father just came back from the US. He spoke English at home. Then sometimes he had his friends at home. At that time, I could speak English, too. I would even chat with my father's friends. (Moya, 1st interview)

Apart from providing material support and creating learning opportunities, one of the most common ways for the participants' parents to become involved in their language learning was to finance private English tuition classes for them. Attending private English classes seemed to be a strategy for parents to give the participants extended language exposure, enhance their interest and increase their confidence in learning English:

> But a friend of my parents, she was an English teacher. She taught me ABC when I was nine. (Yaojing, English original, 1st interview)

> When I was very small, my mother took me to a private language class called 'Hong Kong English'. They used Hong Kong's textbooks.

> There was a teacher from Hong Kong teaching us. [...] I learnt a lot of vocabulary and became very interested in learning English. The teacher also praised me. And I became very confident. (Jing, 1st interview)

Yaojing also shared another reflection on her experience at a private English school in Beijing in the interview:

> I can remember a teacher from ABC school because he is so different from teachers I met in the high school. He knew a lot. [...] I came to know that the English language is a vast ocean. He could tell you that some words are close to each other. Yet there could also be many differences in their meanings. It is a very special experience of learning English. (Yaojing, English original, 1st interview)

Apparently, the courses taught by private tutors helped Yaojing to reflect on their approaches to learning English. In other words, these parents used private English classes and recruited other social agents, English teachers, to positively mediate the participants' development as language learners.

Direct involvement in the participants' learning

Seven participants revealed that their parents were directly involved in their English learning. It was not a surprise that those parents who were English teachers themselves should start teaching their children the English language and show them how to learn English when they were young. However, those parents who did not necessarily have professional knowledge of language learning and teaching also gave suggestions to guide their child's learning and strategy use. Jessy's mother, who presumably drew from her own past learning experiences, insisted that the participant should listen to an audio cassette again and again until she had made progress in her listening comprehension:

> [...] at junior middle school, I was not good at listening comprehension. My mother told me to write down a sentence after listening to it. If I got it wrong, I needed to listen to it again and then write it again. I kept doing it for a month. My listening comprehension improved. (Jessy, 1st interview)

Liu's father, who knew little English but tried his best to keep up-to-date about recent developments in English learning and teaching in China, provided critical guidance for her in how to learn English:

Gao: You look as though you have been learning English for a long time. When did you start?

Liu: Well, I have quite a lot of knowledge about it (how to learn English). I did spend a lot of time on finding out how to learn it. Well, actually, I did not. It was my father. Although he was not good at English at all, he read widely in this area. I think that he was as good as a researcher on how to learn English. In fact, he knows little English. He did not even know how to figure out the twenty-six letters (Liu, 1st interview)

While these parents made various attempts to improve their child's language learning, two participants obviously had over-zealous parents who tried to force them to develop certain strategies due to their convictions regarding language learning. Yu, whose parents were convinced that she should start memorizing English vocabulary as soon as possible, was forced to memorize words at a young age. The experiences of memorizing difficult words by rote for Yu were not happy ones and made language learning a burden to her.

[…] he believed that I should start learning English at a very young age, but his method, I feel, is totally wrong! From the very start, he asked me to memorize and recite words. He asked me to memorize many many words. Because I finished all the words for the junior and senior school English, he asked me to memorize words for the second year college students when I WAS STILL IN PRIMARY SCHOOL. By memorization, I mean, if you ask, I should be able to tell you a particular word's meaning. Well, in fact, I do not think that I remember all of them. (Yu, 1st interview)

Four participants were lucky to have parents who were tactful in encouraging their use of particular learning strategies. The parents had involved themselves closely in the participants' learning by being with them and attending to the affective aspect of the participants' language learning and strategy use, which helped induce changes in their strategy use and the adoption of certain language learning beliefs. For instance, Ran Ran's strategy of learning English by listening to English music might have been a purposeful action or the accidental result of a hobby shared by the mother and the child learner: both of them liked to listen to English songs on the radio:

During my junior middle school days, I began to like to listen to the radio (English by China Central Radio Station). Well, it was actually year 2 at my junior middle school. At that time, my mother started it. My mother liked English songs very much. Just because we wanted to listen to English songs so much, we began to listen (to the English radio) in Year 2 at my middle school. [...] Later, I listened to it even at daytime. [...] it often had five-minute news each hour. And I listened without turning it off. I did not understand it very well in the beginning. Later at senior high school, [...] I could understand quite a lot. (Ran Ran, 1st interview)

In short, the inquiry revealed that Chinese parents (and other members of the family) were as closely involved in the participants' English language learning development as they were in their academic development, playing crucial supporting and guiding roles. Their involvement left a profound impact on the participants' discourses about learning English, material conditions for learning English and development as language learners in terms of strategy use. The study confirmed that the participants' family tried to foster positive learning attitudes and values among them and helped them to internalize a motivating learning discourse that relates the learning of English to both material gains and their desired social identities. In addition, some participants were exposed to the target culture through their parents and other relatives. As a result, the participants' families also directly left marks on their strategy use and learning beliefs. Such family involvement played an important role in the participants' development as language learners, something which cannot and should not be neglected by researchers.

Teachers as significant others

In most research literature on learner development or training studies (Wenden, 1998, 2002), teachers often appear to be the undisputed givers or facilitators, who either lead or assist language learners in the process of learners' strategy development. The data suggest that English teachers had a similarly important role in mediating the participants' discourses about language learning and strategy use (see Table 4.5).

Like parents, teachers in all the participants' formal school settings emphasized the importance of learning English, pressed them to devote time and energy to doing so or improving specific English skills for examinations and tried to create opportunities for them to use relevant learning strategies. Since the English language was always one of the core academic subjects for the participants in their schools, two participants mentioned that their teachers were often seen working together with their parents to shape their discourses about learning English, convincing them that the

Table 4.5 Teachers' mediation on the participants' development as language learners (*N* = 21)

No.	*At the level of*	*Mediation*	*Numbers*
1	Learning discourses	Instrumental value of English and the importance of learning English	21
2	Involvement in learners' strategic learning process	Foster or impose certain learning strategies, i.e. memorization and learning for examinations	21
3	Learning discourses	Encourage learners' reflections on learning	At least 3
4	Involvement in learners' strategic learning process	Encourage learners to adopt alternative strategies, such as reading for pleasure	At least 3

English language would be important to them in the future, usually by emphasizing its instrumental value:

> At secondary school, my teachers and parents all told me that I must learn English well because it would be useful to me in the future. (Ran Ran, 1st interview)

Although English teachers were much more directly involved in the participants' learning in the educational process than anyone else, surprisingly they were not remembered by the participants as powerful figures who dictated how they should learn English. English teachers in the participants' learning past might have tried to tread a balanced line between teaching and learning for examinations and knowledge. However, all the participants found that English teaching in their schools often displayed a much stronger orientation towards examinations. For this reason, English teachers were portrayed in the data as somebody urging them to adopt particular strategies to improve their English examination results as can be seen in the following extracts:

> We had exercises and simulation papers. We were told to copy words every day by teachers and then had dictations every week. And also one simulation paper after another. (Luonan, 1st interview)

> My teacher at middle school was very responsible. His classes always had the best exam results. He simply did a lot of cramming. (Cheng, 1st interview)

All learning and teaching were for exams. [...] After teaching the text, we were told to work on exercises and memorize words. Then we had quizzes and exams. We had to finish a certain number of reading comprehension exercises, clozes and so on. Then we did have classroom performance opportunities. Not many. Most of the time, teachers would explain why we should answer this question this way. We focused a lot on grammar (Jing, 1st interview)

Teachers' teaching approaches, reflecting the imprints of cultural traditions and contextual realities, mediated the participants' ways of learning. As an example, the popularity of memorization strategies among the participants might have been associated with teachers' insistence on memorization in the learning process; the teachers probably found it useful because of traditional exam-oriented learning (Elman, 2000; Lee, W., 1996; Lee, H., 2000) and increasingly competitive educational realities (Miyazaki, 1976; Phelps, 2005). Rachel and Liu recalled their learning experiences associated with memorization activities imposed by their teachers as follows:

He was an old-fashioned type of teacher. He always focused on grammar. If I had any mistake in my homework or exams, I had to go to his office and memorize the right answers before him until I could retell them without any problem. I could not go home until I could do it, even it was eight or nine o'clock in the evening. Everyone in the class would have to memorize those right answers before they could go home. (Rachel, 1st interview)

In my third year at junior middle school, the teacher told us that we had to understand thoroughly what we had learnt today. We had to memorize and recite every text to him [...] I think that memorization was good because it kept you speaking English and reading English to maintain the feel of English. (Liu, 1st interview)

Teachers were especially active in preparing students for the examinations by getting them to work on exam-related exercises, a phenomenon noted by all the participants. At the height of such exam preparation, teachers decided what kind of exercises and learning activities the participants should work on in learning English by weighing up the relative stakes of different examinations. In the following extracts, Cheng and Jingwei described how they were urged to do exam-related preparations:

Because we had essay writing in exams in middle school, we were required to do some exercises related to writing. Sometimes, our teachers would purposefully select certain exercises to improve our writing competence. They were mainly related to grammar. It seemed that an increase in vocabulary had little to do with our writing improvement. (Cheng, 1st interview)

I remember that teachers at senior high school would give us many reading comprehension materials. Those short paragraphs with questions. After reading these materials, I did not have time for reading other materials. (Jingwei, 1st interview)

In spite of the focus on examinations and memorization, the data suggest that a few teachers (at least in the accounts of Meng, Tianzhou and Dongxu) did attempt to encourage the participants to expand their learning opportunities and use alternative learning strategies when exam-oriented learning needs were not pressing, for instance, during their first year in junior or senior high schools. Unfortunately, most of these measures did not last long either because teachers found them unsustainable or because examinations became a critical issue for teachers and students in later years, also revealing the contextual constraints on the participants' language learning and strategy use:

An English teacher asked us to write English journals. After we had written for a while, he told us that he could not read all of them and told us not to write any more. (Meng, 1st interview)

He encouraged us to read extensively. He would often select some interesting stories for us to read. This happened in the first and second years at senior high school. [...] It was really a fun time. (Tianzhou, 1st interview)

(In the first year at senior high school), the teacher did not focus on grammar points. He would try to organize us to prepare for an English drama. He thought that it was much more important for us to increase our real competence. [...] However, my class always had the worst English exam results. [...] in the second and third year, the school put all students with good exam results in one class, called 'the experiment class'. (Dongxu, 1st interview)

Although the study participants were winners in the ruthless academic competition that their teachers had prepared them for, they were nevertheless quite critical of the ways in which teachers organized their English learning in the school. They expressed their dissatisfaction, even disdain, in interviews when they referred to their experiences of learning English at secondary schools, indicating that purely exam-oriented lessons did not help them to improve their real English competence. Possibly for this reason, many of them, supported by their parents, took part-time English classes after school. However, they were apparently unable to get rid of the habit of learning for examinations as many of the out-of-class courses taken by these participants also prepared them for English examinations, such as IELTS or TOEFL. Surprisingly, at least three participants including Moya found that their after-hours teachers could help them to learn English or think about learning English in a different way, as mentioned in the earlier section on family involvement, leading to some reformulation of learning beliefs among the participants:

> [...] he not only taught what was in the book, he also talked about many other things. He used a lot of jokes. All those jokes were related to English. He would tell us good sentence examples. It made me feel that the way we used to learn English was a blind alley. He said that it surely would not work. I totally agreed with him. (Moya, 1st interview)

Ting also noted that teachers in these part-time schools spoke better English than their school teachers as the schools often purposefully chose those teachers with a good reputation:

> She has been to the US, UK and France. I learnt a lot from her. She was really famous in Beijing. I found that she spoke really good English. I always tried to imitate her ways of speaking. After a year, I made significant progress in learning English. (Ting, 1st interview)

Although teachers in those part-time English courses had more inspiring teaching methods or better subject knowledge, surprisingly they did not appear to make the participants adopt less exam-oriented strategies. In fact, they seemed particularly good at either teaching the participants better strategies to enhance their examination performance or at making them feel that they were ahead of their peers who did not take these part-time courses. This suggests that the participants' criticisms of teachers' exam-oriented teaching at school were more about the quality of the teaching and the perceived opportunities provided by examination success at school, and apparently much less about the exam-oriented learning itself (also see Thøgersen, 2002). Since the participants attended these schools at later stages of their learning on the Chinese mainland, it was likely that they had accepted exam-oriented learning as an essential part of learning that they needed to succeed in, given the extremely competitive educational conditions on the Chinese mainland.

In summary, teachers did make an important contribution to the participants' learning (see Table 4.5). In particular, together with parents, they were strong advocates of English as a language critical to the young people's future. Among all the participants, teachers in their formal school settings were often found to put much emphasis on exam-oriented learning. They urged the participants to take up exam-oriented learning strategies, although some teachers attempted to foster a more expansive learning approach among them if the situation permitted. However, in retrospect, these teachers' mediation on the participants' English learning did not seem to last long after the National College Entrance Examination had been taken. In contrast, many participants found English teachers in part-time courses at private schools inspiring and motivating, often leaving a deep impression on their learning of English. In conclusion, teachers in both formal and informal schools were important agents whose teaching made the participants adopt particular sets of learning strategies and reflect on why they had learnt English in particular ways, in some cases leading to a critical evaluation of teachers' participation in the learning process.

Peer mediation

In the learning process, the participants interacted with other English language learners at schools and universities on the Chinese mainland, in light of the strong culture for mutual collaboration among Chinese learners (Cheng, 2000; Cortazzi & Jin, 1996; Littlewood, 1999). The interview data support the argument that the participants' experiences of learning English and strategy use were mediated by their interaction with peers, although their learning of English was largely done in isolation. Consequently, only three participants in schools and seven during the preparatory year mentioned use of social learning strategies with peers.

In general, all the participants went to the best schools in their places of origin, schools with the highest numbers of graduates entering top universities on the Chinese mainland. They reported that their peers were as motivated to achieve academic success in terms of examination scores as they were. The presence of motivated peers was important for the participants. Although it did not lead to greater peer collaboration, it encouraged them to concentrate their efforts on improving their examination results and made them become highly committed to a strenuous learning process. Only occasionally, at the instigation of some teachers, did they find themselves organizing interesting activities such as drama performance and in-class conversation practices, which required them to collaborate with each other. In the interviews, at least four participants told me that they always had long school days before the National College Entrance Examination and had little time for themselves and friends. According to my knowledge, this was a much more widespread phenomenon among senior high school students on the Chinese mainland and probably explained why the participants did not talk much in the interviews about their experiences of working with peers.

When they did mention experiences of learning with peers, they mostly recalled how they collaborated with their peers to create learning opportunities and try new learning strategies (see Table 4.2). However, their references to their experiences of mutual peer support reflect that the reported incidents of peer collaboration were still overshadowed by a pronounced exam-oriented learning approach in schools, indicating the constraints that the broader learning context had on individual learners and their peer interaction. Moya recalled her experience of memorizing English together with her classmates as follows:

> We had a few friends, who decided to memorize vocabulary together. We each memorized one list of words from a book and then tested each other. If I could memorize more than others, I felt that I had achieved something. I thought that it was fun. Because we tested each other, we had to memorize words seriously. (Moya, 1st interview)

At school, if learners had a good relationship with each other, they would encourage or discourage each other from using alternative strategies. In the case of Meng, whose teacher encouraged them to read more English classic novels, her peers tried to modify the teacher's instructions and persuaded her to read materials that interested her rather than to follow the instructions blindly:

> After we began to read classics, most of my classmates said that it was not fun to read them and told me to stop reading them. They recommended me to read something more popular. And I did so. After all, it was just for entertainment. Who would be able to appreciate classical novels? (Meng, 1st interview)

As examination pressure was a key factor compelling the participants to learn English in isolation, during the preparatory year in mainland Chinese universities, when examination pressure disappeared, the data indicate that more participants had experiences of collaborative learning. Seven participants sought to expand their learning opportunities and managed to find supportive friends to work with them on learning English, especially spoken English:

> I practised English conversation more than other skills because I liked to do it. Well, my classmates would come to practise English with me. If they did not, I would look for them to practise English. [...] I would go to English corners or any other English activities. (Liu, 1st interview)

Five of those who happened to be studying in the same university during the preparatory year, organized themselves into a group and recruited an English teacher, who had been abroad, to give them extra English tuition. Luonan, as one of the group, remembered that they tried to use English among themselves:

> We had a regulation among us. We could not speak more than a certain number of Chinese sentences. Otherwise, we would be fined. It worked on the first day. It did not last longer than two days. (Luonan, 1st interview)

Other participants like Jing also endeavoured to create more learning opportunities so that they could use social strategies to improve their oral competence, such as English corner activities:

> I found it boring for a group of Chinese students to speak English together. After going there for a couple of times, I stopped going there. [...] And they always started talking in Chinese after a while. Although I felt that my pronunciation was good, I just could not express what I wanted to say. (Jing, 1st interview)

However, as noted by Luo and Jing, none of these forms of collaboration lasted long, either because they did not have a strong motivation to persist or because the students were not satisfied with the learning opportunities emerging from such collaboration. Overall, the inquiry produced limited data on the peers' mediation on the participants' learning of English and their strategy use, although this does not negate the importance of peer mediation in the learning process. The examination pressure there was understandably prevalent among the participants as they all learnt in highly competitive educational settings. Nevertheless, the inquiry did record several positive incidents with peers in the participants' interview data. A good relationship with peers often helped the participants to adopt collaborative learning strategies, such as creating new opportunities for using English (e.g. Liu). However, the competitive educational context, which made learning and teaching highly exam-oriented, often constrained peer interaction and limited its positive impact on the participants' strategy use.

Cultural Artefacts (Examinations)

From the sociocultural perspective, learners' socialization process is mediated by social agents using a variety of physical (material) and non-physical artefacts (Donato & McCormick, 1994; Lantolf, 2000; Palfreyman,

2006). Consequently, these artefacts mediate language learners' experiences of learning and strategy use. Previous sections in this chapter, when demonstrating the mediation of various social agents, have already pointed to the connection between the participants' internalization of societal and traditional learning discourses and social agents' mediation practices. For instance, teachers and parents were found to have mediated these discourses to the participants, which in turn became a core part of the participants' motive/belief system underlying their strategy use in learning English. These sections have also documented the mediation of material conditions and cultural artefacts on the participants' strategy use. For example, parents provided good learning materials, facilitating their child's language learning and use of particular strategies, such as reading quality English materials extensively. Among all the artefacts, material or cultural, having an impact on the participants' previous learning experiences, examinations, especially high-stakes examinations, turned out to be the most influential. This had already emerged in the data presented in the earlier sections on teachers' mediation in the participants' language learning efforts. As the present educational competition intensifies, with high social positions and career opportunities becoming increasingly limited in relation to the societal demand, high-stakes examinations have become ever more critical in deciding whether Chinese students' educational investment and efforts are worthwhile. Therefore, it is no surprise that examinations, or learning assessment methods, have turned out to be the most important mediating artefacts in the participants' strategy development process (Table 4.6).

In the data, all the participants complained about how examinations dominated their previous learning experiences at secondary schools on the Chinese mainland. They found themselves preoccupied with learning activities preparing them for high-stakes examinations when learning English on the Chinese mainland, particularly before they took the National College Entrance Examination. They all had to work on simulation exercises in the hope of getting good scores in examinations. Moya's account was representative of the participants' experiences:

Table 4.6 Examinations in the participants' development as language learners ($N = 21$)

No.	*How examinations mediated my language learning?*	*Numbers*
1	Exams dominate my learning	21
2	I do not like to learn for exams	15
3	I once chose to take exam-preparation courses outside school	10

> Starting from the junior middle school, I started doing a lot of exercises. My English grades were good at that time. I felt that I might have poor scores if I did not work on exercises. I would feel very bad about it. In order to have good exam scores, I kept working on exam exercises. At senior high school, I worked on exercises [...]. (Moya, 1st interview)

In such a frenzied exam-oriented learning process, the traditional belief in the capacity of education to change one's life was translated into a belief that good examination results were, from the participants' viewpoint, the means of achieving and maintaining 'elite' social status (Miyazaki, 1976). Ting made the following statement:

> In primary school, only a dozen of the whole class could go to a good middle school while the rest had to go to non-key middle schools. I went to a better middle school so I was able to go to a better senior high school. Among those who went to non-key middle schools, most did not go to university or went to non-key universities or vocational schools or joined the workforce. It made a huge difference for us. (Ting, 1st interview)

Stories indicating that life could be changed due to the status change brought by examination success were repeated in exam-preparation materials widely used by students on the Chinese mainland. Two participants including Luonan described a special set of test preparation materials as one of the most widely used test preparation materials among secondary school students on the Chinese mainland. These materials were popular because of the story behind them: a group of poor but hardworking students used these exercise books to obtain high scores in the National College Entrance Examination and this changed their lives forever. Such stories embodied the popular societal and traditional discourses about education and learning (Miyazaki, 1976; Thøgersen, 2002), made these examination practice materials more reliable and also justified their use in the learning process:

> Almost all schools had this series of exam practice books called 'Zhi Hong You Hua (志红优化)'. 'Zhi Hong' was a special class full of students from poor families who had good academic records (author's note: Zhi Hong literally means 'having revolutionary spirits' or 'being highly committed to a particular cause'). 'You Hua' (optimalization) books were exercises books they used before taking the National exam. [...] The book was widely known among all secondary school students because we all had to take the national exam. (Luonan, 1st interview)

However, the emphasis on exam-oriented learning and teaching at school was not favourably received by the participants, as mentioned earlier. Fifteen participants expressed negative feelings about the exam-oriented learning, most of them finding it boring and painful to learn English in such a manner. Repeated exercises were even discouraging for some participants like Liu who did not like the feeling of being defeated when she often failed to answer half of the multiple choice grammar questions correctly in simulation exercises. In the data, no participant said anything positive about such learning. The following quotes are a few examples that show how critical the participants were of the teaching and learning efforts that were oriented towards taking high-stakes examinations:

> It was all for the National Exam. We worked on exam papers all the time. We worked on multiple choice exam questions all the time. I could only get half of these questions answered correctly. It was really painful. The more I worked on them, the more wrong answers I got. I felt that I had been repeatedly defeated. (Liu, 1st interview)

> Learning English at school is really, well, how to say it, [exam-oriented], since our education always encourages us to learn for the sake of exams. First of all, I was not interested in such a kind of learning. Second, I do not think that it worked. (Zhixuan, 1st interview)

> It was a very boring thing to learn English at school. All classes were for exams. (Jing, 1st interview)

> My teachers at school always told us what kind of English would be tested in exams [...] I felt that it was really boring. (Cheng, 1st interview)

Nevertheless, such experiences did not prevent the participants from using examinations as objective goals when trying to improve their English. Although complaining loudly about exam-oriented teaching at school, 10 participants took examination preparation courses outside school. When they felt less pressurized by examinations during their preparatory year, they seemed more willing to use alternative strategies, which appeared to be less related to achieving examination success. Yet, six participants, including Jessy, took exam-preparation courses during the year after they finished the National College Entrance Examination. They reported using international English language proficiency tests such as TOEFL or IELTS to guide their English learning:

> When I was at Peking University, I worked on TOEFL and New Concept English words. I even memorized TOEFL vocabulary. (Jessy, 1st interview)

In short, examinations as artefacts were found to play a dominant role in the participants' development of strategies in learning English on the Chinese mainland. Although they did not enjoy exam-oriented learning and teaching at institutions prior to their tertiary studies in Hong Kong, the data show that they were also ready to use examinations as the embodiment of learning objectives in order to mobilize their learning efforts. Since all the participants were winners in this highly competitive educational system, they had probably been more motivated to learn for examinations before coming to Hong Kong. In other words, although exam-oriented learning and teaching wasted valuable time and made learning and teaching painful for them, it nevertheless enabled them to access better educational and social opportunities by being successful exam-takers. Therefore, the ambiguous attitudes towards examinations actually reflect the mediation of competitive contextual realities and their readiness to use examinations to mobilize their learning efforts should be considered as rational responses in the participants' struggle to be on the top of the social hierarchy through educational efforts.

Agency in the Participants' Strategy Use

The above discussion of the data has highlighted the role of contextual mediation, the prevalent societal and traditional discourses about learning English, social agents' mediation and the significance of high-stakes examinations in the participants' strategy use on the Chinese mainland. While such discussion signifies the importance of contextual conditions in mediating the participants' strategy use, it should not be seen as underestimating the important role of the participants' agency in putting numerous efforts into learning English as documented in the data. Learners' strategy use cannot be properly explained without addressing the issue of agency, which is revealed in their use of power (Giddens, 1976, 1982, 1984).

Firstly, at the core of the participants' strategy use in learning English were their discourses about learning English, which consisted of motivational (values and attitudes) and belief discourses in the interview data. The participants' use of these statements, reflecting what was dominant in the sociocultural context, acted as a vast reserve of discursive resources, to stimulate, regulate and justify their strategy use, particularly after they had acquired and internalized these discourses in the socialization process (Donato & McCormick, 1994; Lantolf, 2000; Thorne, 2005). Although the participants' discourses about learning English resulted from a socialization process mediated by many social agents using a variety of artefacts

(Donato & McCormick, 1994; Parks & Raymond, 2004), such situated agency played a crucial role in motivating and guiding the participants' strategy use towards their desired learning objectives. After all, what is socioculturally appealing and widespread in society, to some extent, must have echoed what is desired by individual participants and become internalized through a process of interpretative reconstruction by them (Corson, 1997; Dean *et al.*, 2006; Layder, 1990).

Secondly, participants' agency was also reflected in the fact that most of them retained their individuality in strategy use regardless of the dominant societal and traditional discourses about learning English and enthusiastic efforts from social agents, including family members, teachers and peers. However, in spite of all the mediation efforts from these social agents, the data suggest that the participants attempted to use appropriate strategies for their learning; and their strategy choices were frequently the result of their own pursuits, albeit mediated by the learning context. In other words, they showed that they had the capacity to 'act otherwise' (Giddens, 1984: 14), although their capacity to act otherwise did not lead to their open resistance to the contextual impositions on their strategy use. The particular patterns of strategy use displayed in the learning accounts were therefore probably the participants' rational responses to the learning environment and indicative of their agency (Sealey & Carter, 2004).

Thirdly, among all the participants' reflections on their strategy use in learning English, they were most dubious of exam-oriented learning efforts and their positive impact on learning English, as indicated in Dongxu's interview extract. They were also able to critically evaluate which strategies they acquired from the socialization process were helpful and which were not. They understood that much of what they had been doing only helped them to achieve examination success and was often meaningless in terms of acquiring better proficiency, confirmed again in the following interview extract:

> We had to do a lot of simulation exam papers every day. We actually spent very little time on learning English. I spent more time on getting myself familiarized with the exam questions and identifying techniques I could use to improve my scores. I do not think that we were learning English at all. We were learning to deal with English exams. (Dongxu, 1st interview)

This indicates that the participants were ready to adopt a different set of strategies once they were allowed to do so by a change in circumstances, a trend in strategy use already captured by Table 4.2. Such reflexivity can be seen as an expression of their agency (Giddens, 1976).

Fourthly, a brief note should be made about the participants' beliefs in learning English as revealed in the data because the preceding arguments suggest that their beliefs about how to learn the language played a role in their language learning (also see Yang, 1999). Although much less present than their references to motives (values and attitudes) in the data, a few participants did talk about what they perceived as appropriate ways of learning English. For instance, participants like Rachel and Ting believed that they should learn English as if they were learning it like a child, while Zhixuan also held the view that it was important for him to memorize a few key English texts as he did the same when learning Chinese. These beliefs led to their use of memorization strategies (in the case of Zhixuan) and strategies to increase their exposure to English (in the case of Rachel). They are indicative of a tendency among these participants to conceive of the learning of English in the same way as the acquisition of their first language. Zhixuan formed his learning beliefs by reflecting on his prior learning experiences, although the data do suggest that personal beliefs were related to the social agents' mediation practices (in the cases of Rachel and Ting). As the data on the participants' personal learning beliefs were limited in the baseline interviews, this issue receives further attention in the later chapters.

Mediation of Contextual Conditions

Apart from highlighting the role of agency, the data recorded some contradictions among the participants between what they preferred to do and what they actually did in the learning process, particularly in relation to exam-oriented learning and teaching. For instance, their negative responses to exam-oriented teaching and learning did not negate their readiness to take measures for improving their examination performance or to use examinations as stimulating goals for regulating their strategy use in learning English. Underlying such ambiguous attitudes towards exam-oriented learning might be a fundamental need among them for objective testimonies of their learning achievements, which could be used to demonstrate their lead over other learners. Such a need could only be properly explained with reference to the contextual realities on the Chinese mainland.

At all times in Chinese history, there have been more demands for opportunities for social advancement than Chinese society has been able to offer. The dynamics in the educational system, including its examination system, on the Chinese mainland, seem to be determined by the harsh demand–supply reality. The Chinese mainland today has inherited a tradition where education, in particular high-stakes examinations, plays a decisive role in determining a student's social mobility (Elman, 2000; Lee, W., 1996; Lee, H., 2000; Miyazaki, 1976; Thøgersen, 2002). Moreover, in spite of two decades of enviable economic progress, the Chinese mainland has witnessed the re-birth of a social hierarchy based on material wealth, the widening gap between the haves and the have-nots and the intensification of competition for social positions in the highest echelons of the social hierarchy (Hu, 2004; Nunan, 2003). What this inquiry has addressed is the phenomenon that in an increasingly stratified society, the well-resourced 'elite' are most willing to commit more material and social resources to their child's educational future, which in turn further confirms the spell of the societal and traditional discourses on the participants' learning of English. As a result, the participants, 'elite' students from socioeconomically advantaged families, still found themselves subject to the necessity to achieve examination success in English, however critical they were of exam-oriented learning. In this sense, the participants' agency in strategy use was constrained by the contextual realities. Meanwhile, their strategy use is indicative of their understanding of the societal and traditional learning discourses as well as contextual realities on the Chinese mainland. For instance, their exam-oriented strategic learning, in particular the popularity of exam-oriented memorization strategies, was facilitated by their awareness of the social reality at large, namely the imbalance of supply and demand of social promotion opportunities.

An Understanding of the Participants' Emerging Strategy Use

An understanding of the ongoing interaction process between agency and context underlying the participants' strategy use emerges from the preceding discussion on agency and contextual conditions (see Figure 2.5). The findings suggest that learners' power, the will and capacity to act otherwise and a precondition to learner agency (Giddens, 1976, 1984), seems to have been profoundly mediated by contextual realities, including social agents, societal and traditional discourses and (material/ cultural) artefacts. In turn, such mediation had a deep impact on their strategy use in learning English. The findings lead to further reflections on what constitutes learner agency in the data, seeing agency in terms of power, or the will and capacity to act otherwise (Giddens, 1984). The data indicate that learners' capacity consists of their knowledge of what strategies are needed to achieve their learning objectives (strategic learning capacity) and a critical understanding of contextual discourses and realities (sociocultural capacity), as well as their competence in utilizing such knowledge and understanding in the learning process. Their will to learn refers to the motive (value/attitude) and belief system emerging from their learning discourses, which were indicative of a strong desire to be successful, whether these discourses were their own beliefs or something that they were urged to endorse. These mutually interactive components formed the core of the participants' power, a precondition to their agency's underlying strategy use in the learning process (Giddens, 1976, 1984). With these capacities and the will to act, the participants were thus able to actively interpret and understand contextual reality, the nature and demands of learning English as a task. Meanwhile, they were able to assimilate further the societal and traditional learning discourses to empower their language learning and regulate their strategy use on the Chinese mainland. Such theorization of learner agency does not exclude the fact that other important factors such as aptitude, learning styles and so on were also at play in influencing the participants' strategy use.

The study did not record that the participants' use of these capacities led to significant events suggestive of their efforts to transform contextual conditions in their pursuit of learning, although a few participants did recall brief experiences of collaborating with each other in their learning pursuits. However, their critical comments on exam-oriented learning and teaching at schools in the interviews demonstrate that they were highly reflective. These comments also indicate that their strategy use consisted of rational responses to a situation where they had to deal with the fundamental issue of academic survival and success in a fiercely competitive educational context. Meanwhile, although most participants might not appear to have made efforts to transform contextual conditions in the learning process, they at least helped reinforce the mediation of contextual realities on their language learning by acting according to their understanding of contextual realities. In addition, given their young age and dependence on other social agents including teachers and parents in the learning process, it was unlikely for them to display open resistance to contextual impositions on their language learning. Hence, the limited data on the participants' micro-political moves, such as creating and sustaining supportive learning networks, did not mean that they lacked the capacity to transform contextual conditions in the learning process. It probably meant that the particular learning contexts and timing were not conducive to their use of micro-political moves.

Conclusion

So far, I have presented the findings related to the participants' strategic learning on the Chinese mainland and discussed how their strategy choices resulted from this interaction between context (such as academic competition) and agency (such as personal ambitions and various capacities). It is important to note that the inquiry covered the participants' 20 years' life experiences. For quite a long time, they tried to understand, construct and internalize what they were exposed to through the mediation of a host of social agents. Over the years, their will and capacity to act otherwise must have increased gradually as they grew up.

These findings are only a partial picture of the interaction between learner agency and contextual conditions underlying the participants' strategic learning efforts. One must bear in mind that each individual participant had unique language learning experiences in a socialization process mediated by a particular set of individual social agents in their respective settings. Individual participants' educational and family settings might differ from each other and their strategy use varied as a result of different socialization processes. For instance, Meng did not have relatives who went abroad and who acquired a good deal of sociocultural knowledge related to English like Zhixuan, Rachel and Moya. Mengshi's parents never forced him to memorize vocabulary in the way that Yu's father did. This said, the picture generated from the analysis of the interview data is indicative of what might be involved in the interaction between learner agency and contextual conditions underlying the participants' strategic learning efforts on the Chinese mainland.

Chapter 5
Learning English in Hong Kong

Chapter 4 described and interpreted the participants' strategy use on the Chinese mainland. While some of the participants participated in a follow-up longitudinal study for two academic years (for details, see Chapter 6), it was also mentioned in the previous chapters that 15 of the participants in Phase 1 were interviewed about their language learning experiences in Hong Kong 20 months later. This chapter reports on the study in Phase 3, which aims to present an overview of the participants' strategic learning efforts in Hong Kong. As mentioned earlier, findings in Phase 1 helped serve as a baseline for comparison with the findings from this study to demonstrate the extent and the ways in which the participants' strategy use shifted after arrival in Hong Kong. To appreciate their shifting strategy use in Hong Kong, I will also draw on the data collected in Phase 1 concerning their perceptions of the new context upon their arrival, which revealed their reasons for choosing Hong Kong as the place for tertiary studies, their preparedness for the challenges ahead and their expected outcomes. In combination with these findings, this chapter interprets the shifts in their strategy use as a group during the two years' stay.

Hong Kong for Mainland Chinese Students

In Phase 1, I asked about the participants' motives for choosing Hong Kong to undertake their undergraduate studies and the challenges facing them in the new context. An analysis of the relevant data revealed that all the participants were attracted to Hong Kong because of its educational quality (Li, 2006; Li & Bray, 2007; Ming Pao, 2006a).

As can be seen in Table 5.1, one of the reasons most frequently quoted by the participants turned out to be the English-medium instruction policy adopted by the university. The data indicate that the reason as to why English-medium instruction was important to them was linked to

Table 5.1 The participants' motives for coming to Hong Kong for tertiary education ($N = 21$)

No.	Motives	No. of participants
1	English-medium instruction	16
2	More opportunities for overseas studies/ employment	13
3	Academic reputation, good-quality teaching and curriculum	11
4	Parents' decisions	7
5	Course preferences	5
6	Other personal reasons, such as 'wanting to have some changes'	4

other motives underlying their decision to study in Hong Kong. Many participants, including those who were about to study in science programmes, intended to pursue further education in English-speaking countries including the United States. They believed that the university, being an English-medium institution, prepared them for further studies abroad in terms of linguistic proficiency and academic competence. Those who intended to pursue business-related degree studies believed that Hong Kong, as an international city in Asia and a bustling business centre in the region, provided valuable internship, overseas exchange and employment opportunities. In these participants' perception, these benefits would give them a competitive edge in the job market upon graduation. Consequently, it is not surprising that they talked about the quality teaching and curriculum available at the university. The university's academic ranking and reputation gave them further confidence that they could consolidate their status as 'elite' students in the future. In other words, they perceived that they could realize the value of quality education in Hong Kong in accordance with Chinese traditional expectations (Bai, 2006; Lee, W., 1996; Lee, H., 2000; Thøgersen, 2002), which were increasingly difficult to pursue on the Chinese mainland.

In addition, some participants mentioned that they had an intrinsic interest in the courses offered by the universities in Hong Kong, while others mentioned that they looked forward to a change of scene after spending so many years on the Chinese mainland (Table 5.1). Seven participants also referred to their parents as the chief decision-makers behind their educational move to Hong Kong. This figure may not reflect the actual level of parental involvement in their decisions about coming to Hong Kong for tertiary studies. In reality, most of the participants needed a large sum of money to cover their educational and living expenses, which could only be provided by their parents.

In relation to their perceived challenges and difficulties in Hong Kong, all the participants mentioned that their English would be insufficient to cope with learning at the university (Table 5.2). This concern must be understood in connection with the fact that most of them used to be top students on the Chinese mainland and wished to remain so in the new academic setting. Whether their English competence was sufficient or not, there was some genuine concern among the participants about their readiness to undertake studies through the medium of English. They were mostly worried that they might not be able to compete with local students in academic studies as local students had been educated in English for a much longer time. As can be seen in Table 5.2, the majority of the participants were concerned that their vocabulary for academic studies would not be adequate. Quite a number of participants felt that they lacked oral proficiency and would not be able to express themselves freely or participate effectively in class. Others were concerned that their reading speed would be a barrier to their acquisition of knowledge. Writing was another concern for those who pursued studies in particular courses such as the social sciences and law.

Table 5.2   Perceived challenges reported by the participants ($N = 21$)

Perceived challenges	No. of participants
Related to English	21
Vocabulary	16
Speaking	8
Reading	6
Writing	5
Listening	1
Related to Cantonese	8
Academic adjustment	9
Daily life adjustment	1

While English was a focus of improvement for all the participants in their studies in Hong Kong, eight of them did feel that Cantonese would be another difficulty for them to overcome, which is in accordance with contextual realities. Such participants were more likely to be taking business, social science and law programmes and were planning to stay in Hong Kong after graduation. They believed that a good command of Cantonese would make it easier for them to mix with local students as they had learned in the preparatory year from senior students from the Chinese mainland that Cantonese was the dominant language on the campus. This indicates that they already had quite a realistic assessment of the linguistic context in Hong Kong before they arrived.

Furthermore, in spite of the challenges and difficulties facing them, most participants wanted to improve their English and acquire a perfect command or near-native level of English during their studies in Hong Kong. Their expectations of learning achievement were so high that only a slight imperfection in respect of accent was an acceptable compromise for them. The following quote exemplifies their learning expectations, applicable not only to speaking but also to writing, reading and listening:

> I hope that I can learn to have conversations with another person in English fluently, even though I speak English with an accent. I can also have a casual conversation with people in English. Then I can use English to make my presentation. It is best that I can make an English presentation without any preparation, an off-hand one. That is to say, I can talk freely in English, although with an accent, and my language and thoughts are clear. (Tian Zhou, 1st interview, translated from Chinese)

It is debatable whether such learning expectations were realistic; it certainly required an enormous amount of effort for the participants to achieve them. However, not all of them had clear action plans for learning English, portending the dissatisfaction resulting from the failure to realize such learning expectations. The following sections aim to show how the participants' strategy use was mediated by the new setting as revealed in their accounts of learning in Hong Kong.

The Study (Phase 3, April–July 2006)

Like the study in Phase 1, the study in Phase 3 (April–July 2006) is also a semi-structured interview study (see Appendix 2) on the participants' language learning experiences with a focus on their strategy use, involving

15 of the 22 participants (see Table 4.1). All but four participants (Rachel, Mengshi, Liu and Yaojing) chose to be interviewed in Chinese. Supported by preliminary findings from Phase 1, the semi-structured interview questions aimed to explore how the participants' strategy use and learning discourses, including motivational and belief discourses, were mediated by contextual discourses, and material (artefact) and social resources. The study in Phase 1 did not generate much data on the participants' own beliefs in respect to how English should be learnt apart from describing how they were persuaded or obliged to use exam-oriented learning strategies. In this study, particular attention was paid to ensure that they talked about their personal learning beliefs. In short, the following research questions were explored:

(1) What were the distinctive features of the participants' strategy use in Hong Kong?
(2) How did these participants come to adopt particular patterns of strategy use as displayed in the data?

The participants were also invited to reflect on the differences in their strategy use and learning motivations in Hong Kong and on the Chinese mainland. These comparisons not only helped me to understand their experiential accounts in Hong Kong better but also validated their learning accounts in Phase 1. Moreover, informed by the interpretative framework (figure 2.5) and preliminary findings from the study in Phase 1, the following questions were also examined when analysing the data from this phase (Phase 3):

(1) How did the participants construct their language learning discursively in terms of motivation (motives or values) and beliefs?
(2) How did social agents mediate their strategy use?
(3) What were the roles of material conditions, cultural artefacts (examinations) or institutional practices (academic studies in the medium of English) in their adjustment of particular learning strategies?

When analysing the interview data, I used an approach similar to that in the study in Phase 1. Guided by the research questions, I constantly compared and questioned different participants' answers and from such a constant questioning and comparing process, thematic relationships among different categories of data, including the participants' strategic efforts, motivational discourses, learning conceptions, perceived learning progress and impressions of learning settings, gradually emerged (Patton, 1990; Strauss & Corbin, 1998). In addition, findings in the first and follow-up studies (Phases 1 and 2) also guided the analysis (Erickson, 2004).

In the process, it became clear that academic studies conducted in English mediated the participants' language learning and strategy use.

The following sections of this chapter are devoted to using the interpretative framework to present the findings through examining their learning experiences in Hong Kong. These sections demonstrate how the participants' strategy use and learning discourses were related to a learning process mediated by societal discourses, social agents, as well as material (artefacts) conditions and the practices associated with these materials and artefacts. All the interview extracts were translated from Chinese unless otherwise stated.

Participants' Strategy Use

As in Phase 1, the participants' references to their strategy use were coded according to the categories of 'voluntary', 'obligatory' and 'others'. Since English was no longer considered a compulsory academic subject, as it was on the Chinese mainland, the 'obligatory' strategies were not reported in the data, even though the participants took compulsory English enhancement courses at the university. The analysis revealed that shifts in their strategy use in Hong Kong continued the trend that had already begun prior to their arrival (see Table 4.2). The repertoire of strategies in Table 5.3 may resemble what they had used on the Chinese mainland, but a fundamental reshuffle in the ways in which they learnt English was also noticeable in the data. The changing context had made their initiative the main driving force for their strategy use in Hong Kong, while a host of social agents, like teachers and parents, both directly urged and indirectly guided them to learn English in ways that best guaranteed exam results for most of the time on the Chinese mainland. Other important changes may include their growing maturity, which made them gain more control of their own learning. As a result, the data reveal several features of their strategic learning efforts in Hong Kong.

Firstly, after arrival in Hong Kong, all the participants attempted to increase their exposure to language input through watching English TV programmes, listening to the English radio and music, reading English books, newspapers and magazines, as well as using English to surf the internet (Table 5.3). These learning efforts were well supported by the material conditions in the new learning environment and were also largely what they planned to do at the start of their stay:

> I watched English movies, listened to English news, read English newspapers. I often read some newspaper articles or books which have some simple words (I think that they are simple and not difficult

Table 5.3 Strategies reported by the participants in Hong Kong

Category	Strategy items	Counts
Voluntary	Watch English TV/movies/play English PC games	15
	Listen to radio/recordings /songs/other materials	15
	Read English magazines or newspaper or materials	15
	Surf English websites	12
	Seek and create opportunities to practise English with others	10
	Writing English diaries/blogs	6
	Murmur to myself	2
Others (specific strategies)	Pay attention to language used during listening and reading	14
	Memorize words by rote memory (look at a word several times)	14
	Memorize English texts/lyrics/sentences	3
	Memorize words/texts in contexts (listening or reading)	12
	Guessing meaning from contexts	5
	Look up new words in dictionaries (paper or electronic)	6
	Write down a new word in a note book	4
	Limit the use of Chinese in learning English	6
	Imitate others in speaking English	3

to use). Sometimes I read those materials. But I read them for interest, not so much for learning English. (Meng, 2nd interview)

For some time, I had been listening to VOA recordings. I have a set of MP3 for practising listening comprehension. I feel that I can improve my listening comprehension if I persistently spend some time listening to them every day. (Dongxu, 2nd interview)

Yu: For a period of time, I tried to…when I found it necessary to read a particular English book, I would seriously take notes […] I took notes of words, a sentence or a word's usage […]
Gao: Apart from taking notes, what else did you do?
Yu: I tried to watch movies in English. All the movies I watched were in English. (Yu, 2nd interview)

Mengshi: Most of the time, I improve my vocabulary. Maybe I improve my listening when watching TV or listening to English.
Gao: How do you improve your vocabulary?
Mengshi: I try various ways like pick up vocabulary from the newspaper and from all kinds of novels, or articles. Sometimes, I learnt vocabulary from IELTS textbooks, last semester and this semester. (Mengshi, English original, 2nd interview)

As can be seen from these extracts, participants like Meng might have done so out of intrinsic interest in the language and its related culture, but others, such as Dongxu, Yu and Mengshi, displayed a clear sense of learning purpose in acquiring linguistic competence. In the process of being exposed to English, they used a variety of strategies, such as taking notes and using a dictionary, to have a better understanding of the materials they had been watching, listening to or reading.

Secondly, during their studies in Hong Kong, 10 participants reported using English with local students, exchange students and even other mainland Chinese students to improve their English, reflecting the increased necessity of using English at the university. However, most participants in the study had little access to social learning opportunities in Hong Kong, which possibly explains why the other five participants remained silent on the same issue. In response, some participants tried to seek and create social opportunities to use English. For instance, five of them, who were involved in the longitudinal follow-up study, had regular English conversations with me for a year or two. For quite some time, Rachel also considered her regular 30-min phone conversation with another Chinese student in a mainland Chinese university the only means of maintaining and improving her oral proficiency:

Gao: How did you spend your thirty minutes (learning English)?
Rachel: The most special thing I did was that I practised English with my classmate in high school. He is now in Tsing Hua University and he is very proficient in English. He is in Beijing and we practised English over the phone […] Not every day but maybe every other day. During the weekend,

> we spent one hour or something. I cannot buy someone to practise English with me on the campus so I had to. (Rachel, English original, 2nd interview)

These strategic learning efforts revealed the agency of highly motivated language learners, but they were also suggestive of the challenges that they had to endure in the new learning context. Unfortunately, such efforts seemed to be of limited scale and might have had a limited impact on a small number of participants' language learning in the participants' perception.

Thirdly, in Hong Kong, the participants' efforts to learn English, which used to be highly structured through the mediation of teachers and parents in the past, apparently became quite disorganized under the pressure from academic studies and many other things. As a general trend, most of the participants seemed to have spent more time learning English in their first half year than in the rest of their stay because they needed to overcome the linguistic barrier and were required to take compulsory English enhancement courses in the first year. Thirteen participants reported having experienced shifts in learning English during those two years due to a variety of reasons, including the completion of compulsory English courses (e.g. Yaojing), time constraints (e.g. Yu and Yuran) and demotivation (e.g. Jingwei). Only a small number of participants claimed that they had managed to spend time learning English regularly throughout their stay in Hong Kong (Rachel and Mengshi):

Gao: Did you try to spend time learning English?
Yuran: I spent little time learning English. I did not have much time for learning English. (Yuran, 2nd interview)

Gao: If you calculate the amount of time you spent learning English in Hong Kong, how much time do you think that you have spent on it?
Yaojing: Learning English? If I have English courses, the workload is two hours a week, or one hour a week. After it, I stopped learning it. (Yaojing, English original, 2nd interview)

Gao: Did you spend extra time learning English apart from your academic studies?
Jing: No. No. I am very lazy. You see. The most I did was watch American TV dramas, like *Sex and the City*, or *Friends*. (Jingwei, 2nd interview)

Fourthly, the data suggest that seven participants' strategy use in learning English regained momentum in the second year. This change seemed to happen after they experienced incidents that made them feel the critical importance of English in their pursuit of non-linguistic objectives, including participation in an interview for exchange studies or a summer intern job. The change was also induced by the fact that many of them began to think about what they were going to do upon graduation. Among all the fluctuations in enthusiasm and efforts for learning English, the strangest phenomenon was that 12 participants had once spent or were planning to spend some weeks memorizing vocabulary again for high-stakes examinations, such as the Graduate Record Examination (GRE), TOEFL or IELTS. Many of them even returned to the Chinese mainland to take exam-preparation courses, including Jing, Yu and Mengshi:

Jing: That summer, I went to take a LSAT course. I found that the course was really useful [...] because LSAT is very difficult and challenging, [...] including vocabulary. It has a very large vocabulary requirement. [...]

Gao: So you were somehow energized in learning English afterwards?

Jing: Yes. I even tried to memorize GRE words. (Jing, 2nd interview)

I did spend three or four hours a week memorizing words. What I memorized was similar to many other people. The Red Book (for GRE). Just keep turning the pages and reading the words on them again and again. (Tianzhou, 2nd interview)

The data indicate that the participants undertook such examination preparation, usually involving the use of intensive vocabulary memorization, out of a feeling of uncertainty regarding their future, rather than a conviction of the utility of these efforts in the learning of English. On the Chinese mainland, they were more inclined to be critical about their exam-oriented memorization efforts in schools and attribute them to the learning process mediated by social agents including teachers and parents. Nevertheless, a few participants did voluntarily take preparation courses for international English proficiency examinations, such as TOEFL and IELTS, during their pre-Hong Kong year. In contrast, the data suggest that in Hong Kong, these examination preparations had more practical applications as the participants related successful examination results to possible graduate studies in English-medium universities, an alternative to graduate employment. A few participants for some time did think that such memorization efforts would help them to improve their command of English significantly in a short time (e.g. Yuran, Tianzhou, Jeff, Yu, Meng and Jing). To some extent, these participants converted these examinations into inspiring learning goals to mobilize their intensive learning efforts, which would otherwise lose momentum. In other words, high-profile examinations continued to be an artefact used by the participants to regulate their strategic learning efforts.

In brief, after arrival in Hong Kong, they experienced increased exposure to English and were encouraged to use a variety of learning strategies, revealing the positive mediation of the new learning environment on their language learning. However, most participants reported great difficulty in investing regular time and efforts in acquiring linguistic competence, including those longitudinal study participants who regularly shared their language learning experiences with me. In particular, they did not have satisfactory experiences in improving their oral competence through social interaction, which might have seriously undermined their sense of achievement in learning English and in turn, their motivation to learn it.

Participants' Discourses of Learning English

Having described the overall picture of the participants' strategy use in learning English, this section focuses on the participants' discourses about language learning underlying their strategy use. The interview data on the participants' discourses about learning in this study were concerned with their motivational discourses (values and attitudes) (Table 5.4) as well as their learning beliefs (conceptions of learning) (Table 5.6) in Hong Kong. As revealed in the data, the participants' learning discourses indicate that they further internalized the traditional learning discourses that see learning as 'investment' (Bai, 2006; Norton Peirce, 1995). The power of the traditional learning discourses in their language learning might have been reinforced by their exposure to the societal discourses in the new context. Meanwhile, their learning discourses began to display new features as mediated by their learning experiences in Hong Kong. The following interview extract from Tianzhou well captures the general mood among them:

Table 5.4   The participants' motivational discourses ($N = 15$)

No.	Motivational discourses	Numbers
1	Culturally oriented motivational discourses	13
	Relating English to self-assertion	7
	Relating English to cultural experiences	4
2	Instrumentally oriented motivational discourses	15

Gao: Do you think that there are any changes in the motives for
            learning English after you came to Hong Kong from the
            Chinese mainland?
Tianzhou: If talking about changes, I should say that I was enslaved by
            the target I was supposed to accomplish before. It distorted
            the real meaning of learning English. (Gao: What distorted the
            real meaning of learning English?) The College Entrance
            Exams! I don't have to do any learning for today because of
            any external requirements. That is to say, I really can learn
            what I think it is necessary to learn. (Tianzhou, 2nd interview)

As indicated by Tianzhou, the shifting motivational discourses were also
followed by an increasing awareness among the participants that they
could act according to their own preferences, that is, their own beliefs, in
the learning process.

Shifting motivational discourses

Informed by Gao *et al.*'s (2004, 2007) differentiation of cultural and
instrumental motivation among Chinese students, the analysis of data
related to the participants' motivational discourses and identified a mixture of instrumental and cultural motivational discourses, with the latter
becoming increasingly present in the data (Table 5.4).

Furthermore, a dynamic picture of the participants' motivational discourses also emerged from the process of comparing the interview data of
14 participants who were interviewed in Phases 1 and 3. Table 5.5 highlights the most visible changes in their motivational discourses after
arrival in Hong Kong, in addition to the fact that all the participants recognized the instrumental value of English in their educational experiences in
two contexts. Apart from revealing changes in the participants' motivational components, their motivational discourses indicate a gradual shift,
signifying that the sources of motivation became increasingly *self-originating*
rather than *context-regulated* after arrival in Hong Kong. In other words,
most participants in Phase 1 reported being urged to internalize the societal and traditional learning discourses, especially when they were young,
so that they could rely on them to mobilize their learning efforts on the
Chinese mainland. In contrast, they appeared to have become more self-
motivated in Hong Kong as many participants apparently drew on their
internalized motivational discourses to construct what was required of
them in the new learning context. Quite a few participants' motivational
discourses also appear to be more culturally oriented (see Table 5.5).
In many senses, these shifts in the participants' motivational discourses

Table 5.5 Shifting motivational discourses ($N = 14$)

Name	Chinese mainland	Hong Kong
1. Luonan *female arts student*	Disliked learning English	Increasingly interested in it for itself
2. Dongxu *female business student*	English as a means to achieve practical objectives	
3. Yuran *male science student*	Learnt English for practical purposes, such as understanding lectures	
4. Amy, *female business student*	English was an important skill	
5. Meng *female science student*	Had a strong interest in the language itself	
6. Tian Zhou *male business student*	English as an academic subject	Growing interest in undertaking cultural activities in English
7. Jeff *male architecture student*	English as an academic subject	The importance of English in self-expression
8. Mengshi *male business student*	English as an academic subject	Relating English to his identity
9. Yu *female architecture student*	English as an academic subject	English important in asserting herself
10. Yaojing *female science student*	English as an academic subject	English important in learning about cultures and self-expression
11. Rachel *female business student*	English as an academic subject	Growing interest, English as a means to express herself
12. Jing *female law student*	A strong interest in the language and its culture	English was important to her pursuit of self-expression
13. Liu *female business student*	Related English to her identity as an elite student	The link between English and her identity was further strengthened
14. Zhixuan *male science student*	A strong interest in American culture	Continued to be interested in the culture, English and his self-identity

Source: From Gao, X. (2008b) Shifting motivational discourses among mainland Chinese students in an English medium tertiary institution in Hong Kong: A longitudinal inquiry. *Studies in Higher Education* 33 (5), 599–614. Reprinted by permission of the publisher (Taylor & Francis Ltd).

were mediated by the changing contexts. For instance, the English language was no longer a compulsory academic subject as it was on the Chinese mainland, although they all took compulsory English enhancement courses at the university. Neither were there social agents like parents and teachers who used to explicitly mediate and reinforce the societal discourses about learning English to the participants.

Cultural motivational discourses

As the participants became the locus of control in learning English in Hong Kong, nine participants were found to either display additional, culturally oriented motives for learning English or change their attitudes towards learning the language (Table 5.5). For them, English was no longer only a compulsory academic subject for examination. Luonan described the changes as follows:

> When I was on the Chinese mainland, I was really depressed by it. I was not interested in learning it at all. I was forced to learn English. [...] at least, when I first came to Hong Kong, I was very much against learning English. Now, I am no longer against learning English. I found that it was really necessary for me to learn English and tried to have pleasure in the process. (Luonan, 2nd interview)

Even those participants who were 'forced' to learn more English to cope with English-medium coursework had their personal agenda. For instance, Yu had to defend her architectural designs before others regularly in English and for this reason she tried to seek opportunities to improve her oral proficiency (for more details, see Yu's case study in Chapter 6). As a matter of fact, she was one of the most regular participants in the weekly English conversation I had with my longitudinal participants, regardless of her heavy workload. She admitted that she was particularly motivated by a desire to maintain face before her group mates who had a better command of English:

Gao: What caused you to learn English in Hong Kong?
Yu: I was forced to do so. I had no choice. And also there is nothing wrong with learning English here. I guess that I did not want to lose face before others. When you have people around you who can speak terrific English and you feel that your English is so inadequate, you need to change this. Especially in those oral English presentations, if your English is too weak to defend your work, you will be caught up there saying things that you do not understand yourself. (Yu, 2nd interview)

At least five participants including Yaojing were planning to undertake further studies abroad. English was understandably important because they had to pass high-stakes English proficiency examinations and would need English during their future studies. Nevertheless, they were also partially motivated by cultural incentives. For instance, Yaojing appreciated the fact that a better command of English would help her to understand other countries and cultures even though the primary reason she gave for her strategy use in learning English was instrumental:

Gao: So in what ways is English important to you?
Yaojing: Doing postgraduate studies.
Gao: Life is much larger than postgraduate studies.
Yaojing: My future career will be teaching in the university. Academic study will be the major part of my life. If I am good at English, I can have a better understanding of other countries and other cultures, if I travel around the world. (Yaojing, English original, 2nd interview)

The data also reveal that seven participants particularly appreciated the important role that English could play in their efforts to assert themselves. These participants shared a strong desire to express themselves in English. Rachel described such changes in her learning motivation after she graduated from her high school, knowing that she would come to study in Hong Kong:

When I was on the Chinese mainland, I thought I wanted to improve my English because I wanted to achieve a certain level because I know teaching at the university would be conducted in English. Now English is not the means for me to get higher grades. Actually, if you are poor at English, you can still have higher grades at the university. It is more a means for me to express myself to more people. (Rachel, English original, 2nd interview)

Similarly, Jeff who intended to pursue overseas studies and then work abroad as an architect, explained why English was important in future, relating English to his desire for self-assertion. Likewise, Yaojing believed that a good command of oral English was critical to her for becoming the person she aspired to be:

Jeff: Because I intended to stay there for quite a long time, [...] I feel that communication ability, that is to express my thoughts accurately, is very important.
Gao: So you want to become integrated into the community there?

Jeff: Well, I think that it takes a very long time for me to become
                part of the community. What I meant to say is mainly that I
                need to express myself (in English). (Jeff, 2nd interview)

Because speaking, it is a way for other people to have the first impression of you. [...] we can have better communication. And a better,
well, it is easier for me to be part of the student community. Speaking
English identifies you as students with better education. (Yaojing,
English original, 2nd interview)

In short, the interview data show that the participants' motivational discourses became more culturally oriented. However, it is noticeable that
some of the interview extracts in this section (Yu, Yaojing and Rachel's) are
also indicative of the instrumental value of English held by the participants.

Instrumental motivational discourses

The interview data confirm that instrumental motives remained one of
the most important forces driving the participants to invest more time and
strategy use in learning English. When talking about why they had to
learn English in Hong Kong, all the participants referred to the necessity
of surviving and succeeding in an English-medium instruction setting
(e.g. Yuran and Zhixuan), seeking employment upon graduation (e.g.
Mengshi and Jing) and applying for further studies abroad (e.g. Jingwei
and Yaojing). As an example, Yuran related the learning of English to his
academic studies:

Gao: If you do spend time learning English in Hong Kong, what
                has caused you to do so?
Yuran: If I don't do so, well, I do not have an average level of
                English that other students have. If I wanted to catch up
                with others in academic work, I had to learn English. If you
                don't, you cannot understand your lectures, can't write
                properly. [...] Moreover, in the future, you will have to look
                for jobs. To find jobs, you must improve your English.
                (Yuran, 2nd interview)

Moreover, the importance of speaking in the participants' motivational
discourses might also be seen as being closely associated with the medium
of instruction at the university. In the case of Yu, who found herself compelled to defend her design works before her peers in English, it was also
her desire to be successful in her academic studies that pushed her to put
more effort into acquiring spoken English competence.

Learning beliefs (conceptions)

The study in Phase 1 did not explicitly deal with the participants' personal learning beliefs because the participants were more inclined to describe how they were exposed to particular motivational and belief discourses, especially exam-oriented learning ones. Although they might have endorsed these discourses when they were preparing for high-stakes examinations, they were apparently critical of them afterwards, making it uncertain whether such statements should really be coded as their own beliefs guiding their strategy use. In this phase (Phase 3), contextual changes made it necessary for the participants to exert learning efforts according to their own motives and beliefs. As a result, the data generated in the third phase enabled me to undertake a careful examination of the participants' learning beliefs or their learning conceptions.

The interview data reveal that at least seven participants gave top priority to vocabulary, indicative of a quantitative conception of learning (Table 5.6), which considers learning to be 'an increase in knowledge' (Benson & Lor, 1999: 465). This finding is consistent with their use of memorization strategies at the university, especially among those who spent time preparing for high-stakes examinations:

Gao: What do you associate with the idea of learning English?
Jingwei: I can only think of memorizing vocabulary. (Jingwei, translated from Chinese)

I think that it is essential to memorize words. At least, it is most basic and fundamental. Then, you need to improve your language use capacity, in writing essays, [...] how to write a good essay, report, or CV, or even give a good presentation. (Tianzhou, 2nd interview)

Meanwhile, their beliefs in learning English had become more flexible after their arrival because of the availability of English learning resources in Hong Kong. The material learning conditions supported the belief that

Table 5.6   The participants' beliefs (conceptions) (*N* = 15)

No.	*How important is English and how should it be learnt?*	*Numbers*
1	Give priority to vocabulary	7
2	Accents are important	2
3	Exams as an important part of learning	5

English could be acquired through immersion like a child being exposed to natural language input. However, while enjoying activities such as watching movies, which helped them to learn English and to relax after academic studies, at least three participants (e.g. Yuka, Zhixuan and Yu) among those who appeared to emphasize less the importance of memorizing vocabulary mentioned that they also paid considerable attention to the English vocabulary and grammar used in movies and English programmes:

> Everything related to English, including those activities that are often considered learning English, like watching movies and reading novels. [...] I focused on vocabulary, grammar and a feeling of English. For instance, reading a short piece of writing [...]. (Yuka, 2nd interview)

The importance of having a large vocabulary for these participants was self-explanatory as they had to struggle with academic studies in English with vocabulary deficiency being the most persistent barrier, a concern expressed by the participants two years ago (see Table 5.2). Moreover, memorizing vocabulary was more than a cognitive process to retain more words for academic studies: it may also have helped participants like Tianzhou to improve their communicative competence and their ability to assert themselves as vocabulary was an 'essential' condition prior to the use of English on an occasion, as when writing a CV or making a presentation.

Two participants particularly mentioned the importance of acquiring a good accent in learning English:

> I take a holistic perspective on learning languages. [But] accent, accent is very important. (Jing, 2nd interview)

Good accents might have been associated with the perceived need to present themselves in English at the university and in future as Yaojing also regarded 'speaking' as 'a way for other people' to have impressions of the participants.

In addition, five participants (e.g. Jing and Tianzhou) considered preparations for high-stakes examinations an important part of their efforts to acquire linguistic competence. Although not all the participants valued the importance of examinations in learning English in Hong Kong, the data show that examinations still visibly mediated their language learning. Luonan related the 'serious' notion of learning English to taking courses and learning for examinations:

> If I learn English in a serious manner, I would at least take an IELTS course, or TOEFL course. The teacher would teach me 15 minutes and give us exercises for another 15 minutes. It was how I was taught

when I was young. I believe that this is the only way of serious learning. (Luonan, 2nd interview)

It is probably not surprising that exam-oriented learning had become an important part of their beliefs of what constituted the learning of English. Exam-oriented learning was a major part of their language learning experiences on the Chinese mainland. As a result of an extended exposure, exam-oriented learning probably had become a habit, which was not easy for them to break away from. As a result, even in Hong Kong, many participants also voluntarily used high-stakes examinations to mobilize their learning efforts, however critical they were about exam-oriented learning on the Chinese mainland.

Motivational discourses, beliefs and contextual mediation

So far, these findings suggest that the participants' motivational discourses became more multi-faceted with increasingly marked cultural motives in the data, in comparison with the dominance of instrumental motives identified in Phase 1. To some extent, the participants' motivational discourses echo the popular discourses around learning English in Hong Kong's society (Davison & Lai, 2007; Keung, 2006; Morrison & Lui, 2002). English is promoted as an important asset to project Hong Kong's image as an international city in Asia and English competence remains an important employee selection criterion in the business sector. These findings are also indicative of traditional learning discourses in which learning has both instrumental and intrinsic values (Bai, 2005; Lee, W., 1996; Lee, H., 2000; Miyazaki, 1976). Probably in Hong Kong it became more obvious to the participants that such instrumental value of English could be realized as many of them saw Hong Kong as a city of opportunities, which was one of the most important incentives attracting them to come. Meanwhile, their increased exposure to the language and its cultural products, especially opportunities to use English meaningfully for academic and social purposes, apparently fostered strong cultural motives among them (see the interview extracts of Luonan, Yu and Rachel). They were also one step closer to the realization of a vision in which they saw themselves as global travellers (see the interview extracts of Yaojing and Jeff), affirming the importance of English in their effort to attain desirable identities. In other words, their experiences had probably mediated their further internalization of a mixture of traditional learning discourses, reinforced by the societal discourses in Hong Kong. As a result, their motivational discourses became more multi-faceted (Gao, 2008b).

The interview data provided additional information about the participants' beliefs regarding language learning as a task in Hong Kong. Their previous learning experiences had socialized them into beliefs which encouraged them to focus on vocabulary and adopt strategies more commonly associated with quantitative notions of learning English (Benson & Lor, 1999). There were at least two participants who emphasized the importance of accents, relating their language learning to self-assertion in accordance with the contextual realities and traditional expectations of education (Lee, W., 1996; Lee, H., 2000; Thøgersen, 2002).

In short, these findings also support the argument that the participants' discourses about language learning were closely associated with contextual mediation from the sociocultural perspective (Donato & McCormick, 1994; Palfreyman, 2006). This chapter now goes on to examine their perceptions of the learning context to identify how social agents and material (artefacts) conditions mediated the participants' language learning and strategy use.

Contextual Mediation on the Participants' Strategy Use

Having elaborated on the participants' learning discourses, in this section I explore how social agents and material (artefacts) conditions mediated the participants' language learning and strategy use as reflected in the data (Donato & McCormick, 1994; Parks & Raymond, 2004; Palfreyman, 2006).

From an analysis of the data related to mediating agents (social resources) as well as material and artefacts together with the participants' related sociocultural practices, three themes emerged from the analysis: firstly, peers were an important source of mediation shaping their efforts to acquire English (Park & Raymond, 2004). Secondly, the abundance of English resources available (material conditions) enabled the participants to adopt a variety of new strategies (Palfreyman, 2006). Thirdly, they often had to cope with the conflicting needs of academic studies and learning English, leading to shifts in their strategy use. Academic studies through the medium of English, like English examinations in the past, were found to be an important source of mediation for the participants' strategy use. Further attention was paid in the analysis to sub-coding the relevant data in terms of the mediation on the levels of learning discourses and strategy use. While the mediating agents (peers) were also found to provide material learning resources to the participants, their contributions in this regard were much less significant in comparison with what their parents had done for them on the Chinese mainland and what the university as an English-medium university provided them with in Hong Kong. Hence, peers' contributions in terms of material resources were reported together with their mediation on the participants' strategy use and learning discourses.

Mediating agents: Peers

In Phase 1, the data reveal the important role of various social agents, including parents, teachers and peers, in the participants' learning process. These social agents not only mediated the participants' strategy use but also shaped their learning discourses. After arrival in Hong Kong, they moved away from their parents' close supervision and, at the university, there was no longer a closely bonded relationship between students and teachers in comparison with that in school settings on the Chinese mainland. Therefore, peers emerged as the most important social agents in influencing the participants' learning process in Hong Kong.

Since the university had many students and staff members proficient in English, 10 participants attempted to take advantage of the rich social resources to use social learning strategies and benefit their English learning (Table 5.7). Only one participant (Zhixuan) was absolutely determined not to mix with local students so as to avoid speaking Cantonese, but he

Table 5.7 Peer mediation on the participants ($N = 15$)

No.	Peer mediation	Numbers	Remarks
1	Attempts to use social learning strategies with peers	10	
2	Learning Cantonese to socialize with local students	12	Nine became less enthusiastic about learning English in the 2nd year
3	Socialization with local students to use social learning strategies	3	
4	Receive support for exam-oriented learning from other mainland students	7	
5	Socialize with mainland students to use social learning strategies	5	
6	Socialize with non-local students to use social learning strategies	1	

managed to make a few friends among exchange students and international school graduates in English (for details, see his case study in Chapter 6). Three participants who mainly socialized with local students also managed to gain opportunities for acquiring English competence through social learning.

Far more importantly, one or two participants experienced shifts in their motives and beliefs in learning English as a result of their interaction with peers. Luonan, who was an active executive committee member in a student society and could not speak Cantonese, found it necessary to use English to interact with local student members who could not speak Putonghua. This experience actually changed the negative attitudes she had towards learning English on the Chinese mainland and made her become more interested in learning English. Moreover, her friends became a valuable source of encouragement for her to read more in English:

> In the beginning, I relied on an interpreter to interact with local students. She is also a committee member. She is from Taiwan and can speak Putonghua and Cantonese very well. So she acted as my interpreter. If she was not around, we had to speak Putonghua but Hong Kong students' Putonghua was poor. I cannot understand a word of Cantonese so we had to rely on English, the third language for us to communicate with each other, because we all share the English language. Then gradually, I found that it was a convenient tool for daily life. I realized that I should learn it well. I also had a few good local friends. They grew up in a half-native language environment. They would recommend me to read some English novels, interesting stuff, not like boring textbooks. Because we are all young, we have similar interests in reading. I found what they recommended me to read was really interesting. (Luonan, 2nd interview)

However, two participants (Meng and Rachel) noted motivation for learning English was low among university students and so they felt that Hong Kong was not an ideal place to learn English. They observed that both local students and mainland Chinese students were not willing to spend more time learning English because of the perception that they had already been learning 'in the environment of English' (Rachel, English original). In comparison with motivated English learners in mainland Chinese institutions, Meng felt that there were not enough incentives for students at the university to learn English, which might have reduced their learning motivation (Keung, 2006). In her view, while the presence of motivated students on the Chinese mainland motivated her and other students to learn English, the absence of such motivated students in Hong Kong became a demotivating factor:

> In terms of English-learning resources and facilities, Hong Kong is superior in comparison with those on the Chinese mainland. However, students here are not motivated to learn English, maybe because they have reached certain levels. On the Chinese mainland, good students in good schools are very much motivated to learn English. [...] Here exams are also not valued. (Meng, 2nd interview)

In regard to the participants' language learning experiences, a special note needs to be made about their efforts in learning Cantonese, which may be indicative of the challenges facing them in Hong Kong. While most participants recognized that Hong Kong was a better place to learn English than the Chinese mainland, two participants pointed out that there were limited opportunities to use English as Cantonese was the dominant language for socialization. Jing complained:

> I think that Hong Kong people's English is better than that of mainland Chinese but the gap isn't very big. The most useful language here is Cantonese. Even if I go to the Faculty Office or look for internship opportunities, the language I use for communication and they use for administration is Cantonese. (Jing, 2nd interview)

For this reason, after arrival in Hong Kong, 12 participants tried to learn Cantonese 'for communication' in daily life and academic study situations such as group work (e.g. Mengshi), an integral part of the participants' educational experiences at the university. They learnt Cantonese either because they wanted to build a social network with local students to avoid isolation or because they wanted to express themselves in the medium of Cantonese to meaningfully participate in the student community. Yet 9 out of 12 participants who tried to interact with local students became less enthusiastic about doing so in the second year after a variety of experiences of socializing with local students (Table 5.7). Even though these students shared the same cultural and ethnic roots, they often felt that they were different from local students when they discovered that they had no shared cultural knowledge, as in the case of Yuran, and had different life priorities.

> My relationship with local students is OK. [...] I find it difficult to have some deeper relationship. [...] Not only linguistic difficulty. A lot of barriers were related to our values and perspectives. [...] well, a

lot of things we have grown up with. Something we know but they do not know or they know but we do not know. For example, joking. They cannot understand our joking styles. I cannot understand theirs. (Yuran, 2nd interview)

In addition, they were sometimes uncomfortable with the portrayals of mainland Chinese in Hong Kong's public perceptions as experienced by Jing, although the participants tended to take this issue lightly and some would even blame the mainland Chinese:

Whenever I go to a social occasion and speak English well, they will not say that I am from the mainland. Even if I start speaking Putonghua to them, they still think that I am from some foreign country [...] it makes me feel that they cannot accept a mainland Chinese who speaks good English. Don't you feel this way? [...] I do feel that I have some problems with my identity. [...] When somebody tells me that I am not like a mainland Chinese student at all, this means that he or she has a particular type of mainland Chinese student's image in their minds. Even if you actually praise me, I still feel very bad about it. (Jing, 2nd interview)

None of the mainland Chinese students were able to be re-born with the variety of social and cultural experiences unique to their local counterparts. Consequently, the differences constituted a gap, which may have undermined the social relationship between the two groups of students. As a result, most participants were unlikely to use social strategies in learning English with local students. Participants like Luonan, who changed her motives and attitudes in learning English as a result of her socialization with local students, were rare cases.

As the participants' strategy use, in particular their use of social strategies, might have been discouraged and even frustrated by the lack of local peers with whom they could collaborate to learn more English in the setting, seven participants often looked for other mainland Chinese students for assistance in learning English, in particular when preparing for English examinations (Table 5.7). They circulated ways of preparing for examinations among themselves through the Internet or by word of mouth. For example, those who had prepared for the GRE examination often shared their preparation experiences with those who were planning to prepare for it. Popular preparation methods, including a 17-day vocabulary memorization plan, had been tried, carefully examined and recommended to be the most efficient way of learning English for examinations among mainland Chinese students. Jeff, who was planning to take GRE at the time of the interview, decided to follow the memorization plan, using 'their', that is, his mainland Chinese peers' experiences to justify his decision:

Gao: Are you going to use the 17 day plan?
Jeff: Yes. The shorter the time I spend on memorizing the list, the better. I was told. Every day, I should memorize two or three hundred words in 17 days. They memorized all the words within 17 days. Then they found it was the most efficient way. [...] In fact, I heard that many people memorized the words in this way. Those who did not actually take GRE but tried to memorize words for a month, they decided to give it up halfway because they forgot what they had memorized a month before. If I memorized the words in a very short time, I could remember them at the end of the memorization period, I was told. (Jeff, 2nd interview)

Such peer support not only encouraged them to use exam-oriented learning strategies, in particular memorization strategies, but it also reinforced the mediation of the traditional and societal discourses on their language learning and made the instrumental value of English a prominent theme in their learning discourses. When the participants collaborated with other mainland students in preparation for high-stakes examinations, they drew on the instrumental discourses regarding the learning of English as a means to access further studies in English-medium universities. Apart from advising each other on learning for examinations, the participants reported little collaboration in learning English among mainland Chinese students, except for those who are involved in the longitudinal follow-up study (Table 5.7). For a period of time, longitudinal research participants, including Mengshi and Liu, became conversational partners but similar initiatives to speak English with other fellow mainland Chinese students were rare. Such collaboration potentially reinforced the discourses seeing English as a meaningful way of self-expression between Mengshi and Liu.

Material conditions

In the interviews, the majority of the participants (13 out of 15) referred to the English-learning environment at the university and in Hong Kong in positive terms and made comments similar to the following:

It is a very nice place to learn English. You can find whatever you want to look for, in abundance. There is also a wonderful environment, facilities like the Language Centre. If you want to communicate with foreigners or seek help in learning English, there are many places you can find them. I mean that you can find help or talk to foreigners. (Luonan, 2nd interview)

In general, it is a better place to learn English, at least, I mean the university. [...] In the university, there are many young people, who are well educated. Many of them studied at international schools or went for exchanges. Then students from the Chinese mainland were also good at English. [...] Good facilities, all sorts of English original videos, DVDs and cassettes. A lot of consultation service. Also many newspapers. (Tianzhou, 2nd interview)

In these statements, they acknowledged that learning resources and facilities in the current learning setting were much better than what they had on the Chinese mainland. They pointed out that there were also considerably more English-proficient people to interact with in English as potential social learning resources. The English-medium instruction in the university became an important component of the perceived advantages of Hong Kong as an English-learning environment.

In short, the English learning resources and English-proficient people constituted a favourable learning environment that encouraged and facilitated their strategy use in learning English. As a result, the participants actively attempted to increase their exposure to English and adopt flexible learning approaches. The rich learning resources also encouraged the participants to have cultural learning discourses as they utilized these material resources to learn and use English. Unfortunately, many participants found it difficult to sustain these learning efforts as they became increasingly preoccupied with academic studies.

Academic studies

Apart from referring to the mediation of mediating agents and material conditions on their language learning, the participants reported that academic coursework had mediated their strategy use. For all the participants, academic studies in the medium of English were understandably a factor motivating them to learn more English and became part of their instrumental motivational discourses (see Table 5.8).

While academic studies mediated the participants' learning discourses, four participants in the interviews claimed that they benefited from taking linguistically demanding academic courses because they were encouraged to use a lot of strategies to improve their linguistic competence

Table 5.8 Academic studies and learning English in the participants' perceptions (N = 15)

No.	Academic studies and learning English	Numbers
1	Academic studies made it possible for me to use a variety of strategies	4
	Academic studies helped my English in a very limited fashion	5
2	Difficult to keep a balance between the two	9
	Academic studies made it nearly impossible for me to learn English	2

(see Jingwei's interview extract below). Therefore, they favoured academic learning through the English medium as it became one of the most important means for them to learn more English. In contrast, five participants found that they could only acquire limited linguistic competence through taking academic courses (see Tianzhou as an example). In general, they agreed that academic studies helped them to acquire a certain number of words related to their study area or improve particular aspects of English:

Jingwei: Because the course had weekly assignments, I need to write one piece of reporting every week, a two-minute report. I normally finished it on Monday or Tuesday. Then I would go through it again and again, reflecting on my language use, checking in the dictionary and searching on Google to determine whether a word should be used in this context or not, or whether I had used a word properly. It helped a lot.
Gao: So the course helped you to learn English?
Jingwei: Yes. At least partially. Other courses did not have high requirements for language use so they were not helpful to my language learning. (Jingwei, 2nd interview)

Academic studies only helped me to adapt to lecturers' oral English and improve my listening comprehension. They did not give much help in other areas. Our courses also have a narrow range of words [...] they did not help you to expand your vocabulary much. They helped you to get adjusted to various accents such as Australian accents. (Tianzhou, 2nd interview)

Furthermore, as can be seen in Table 5.8, nine participants commented that it had been extremely difficult for them to manage a balance in academic studies and learning English:

> I did not spend much time learning English. I did not have much time. [...] I got so much to learn for my courses. (Yuran, lines 51–54, translated from Chinese)

> I did take time apart from academic studies to learn English but it was really stressful because you need to cope with academic studies and at the same time spend some extra time learning English. (Jing, 2nd interview)

In some departments, academic study pressure was so high that they missed sleep in order to complete their course assignments. Participants from these departments often had to give up socializing with other students and time for learning English (such as Yu and Jeff). Understandably, under such extreme conditions, regular efforts in learning English could not be sustained, especially among those who felt English was important only for instrumental reasons, such as for helping them to survive academic studies in the medium of English. They quickly lost their enthusiasm once they felt that their English level could enable them to achieve their academic learning objectives; as Rachel pointed out: 'if you are poor at English, you can still have higher grades at the university' (English original). If there was a clash between the need to learn English and to achieve good GPAs for these participants, they would choose to spend time improving academic results rather than learning English (see Gao, 2006a on Chinese students in Britain). Since they learnt English to improve their academic performance through the medium of English, it did not make sense that they should be expected to sacrifice gains in academic studies for gains in English. However, there were also participants like Rachel, though few in number, who did try to devote some extra time to learning English. These participants were often those who saw or began to see that English played an important role in academic studies as well as in their self-assertion or pursuit of their self-identities. They could draw on their multi-faceted motivational discourses to support their ongoing learning efforts.

In short, the inquiry revealed that the participants had mixed socialization experiences with their peers in Hong Kong, which had discouraged and facilitated their strategy use. It also showed that many participants found that academic studies often prevented them from investing time and effort in learning English while some of them claimed that their learning of English benefited from their doing academic studies in the medium of English. These findings indicate that contextual realities, such as the sociopolitical processes that mainland Chinese students had to deal with in Hong Kong, need to be considered when interpreting the mediation of the new learning context on the participants' strategy use in Hong Kong. For instance, being temporary immigrants with an uncertain future status, mainland Chinese students needed to make extra efforts to achieve social promotion in Hong Kong's society compared with their local counterparts. In addition, they lacked the linguistic, social and cultural resources needed to participate meaningfully in the student community due to numerous linguistic, social and cultural differences that they had with local students (Davison & Lai, 2007; Ho *et al.*, 2003; Keung, 2006; Li *et al.*, 1995; Schack & Schack, 2005). As 'elite' mainland Chinese students, they both expected and were expected to realize the value of educational investment, that is, to achieve social promotion and self-improvement (Elman, 2000; Lee, W., 1996; Lee, H., 2000; Thøgersen, 2002). Hence, they had to endure these contextual constraints in seeking and creating opportunities to acquire English while constantly feeling insecure in their learning investment, which were recurring themes in their accounts of language learning and strategy use in Hong Kong.

Overall Learning Progress

Reflecting on these findings, there seem to be some tensions in the participants' expectations of learning achievements and some dissatisfaction with their learning progress. It might be necessary to pay attention to whether they had improved their English by studying in the English-medium university. Given the uncertain nature of the participants' investment in language learning, the data in general do suggest that their decision to study at the university benefited their learning of English in Hong Kong, as there were rich English learning resources and many English users. These changes had encouraged the participants to invest time and strategic efforts in learning English, leading to improvements in their English. Even a modest evaluation was indicative of positive progress as in the following extract:

> [...] improvement was gradual. I do not have feelings of improvement. It is like a child's growth. The child is growing all the time but the parents do not feel it. (Yuka, 2nd interview)

Others were much more positive and reported improvement in specific skill areas, such as writing, reading, listening and/or vocabulary:

> In general, I felt that I have made a lot of improvements in writing and reading. I cannot say that I made much progress in speaking. (Dongxu, 2nd interview)

The participants' dissatisfaction was related to their perceived lack of progress in speaking. While many of them desired to improve their oral competence, it had been challenging for most of them to establish and maintain a language exchange partnership or supportive social learning networks, due to the linguistic and sociocultural complexity on the campus and in Hong Kong. In addition, their learning efforts became quite disorganized and the learning momentum could not be sustained under the pressure from academic studies. Such experiences must have undermined their general satisfaction with the learning progress, leaving their objectives unfulfilled. These findings also indicate that they had to deal with various contextual constraints in their pursuit of linguistic competence in Hong Kong, lending support to the argument that their strategic learning did not pertain to their free will alone but emerged from the interaction with their power, the will and capacity to act (Giddens, 1984), and contextual conditions, such as resources and sociopolitical relationships. The following discussions address the issues of agency and contextual conditions in the participants' strategy use as identified in this study phase.

Enhanced Agency

In comparison with the findings in Phase 1, the participants' agency became a much more pronounced feature of their strategy use over the two-year period. On the one hand, this finding is probably not surprising as they grew more mature and independent over the years. On the other, the inquiry in Phase 1 drew on memories of their youth, when adult figures, including parents and teachers, were quite influential.

After arrival in Hong Kong, the participants not only grew more independent but also found themselves in a new learning context without existing social learning networks. On the Chinese mainland, social agents and contextual conditions had operated as external forces stimulating the participants to work hard on learning English with the societal and traditional learning discourses internalized by them through the social agents' mediation. As a result, the participants' motivational discourses were full of references to the instrumental value of English in alignment with societal and traditional discourses on the Chinese mainland. In Hong Kong, these traditional learning discourses, together with the societal discourses, gradually became internalized as their inner will, revealing the beliefs and values that the participants themselves attached to the learning of English and strategy use. Such changes might have resulted from their increased exposure to social realities as they grew up, regardless of whether or not they studied in Hong Kong, but their educational and social experiences in Hong Kong and the English-medium university also reinforced the mediation of the societal and traditional discourses on their learning. Meanwhile, as the participants' access to English input and production opportunities increased at the university, some participants saw that English competence was essential to their growing desire for self-assertion and identity pursuits and their motivational discourses appeared to be increasingly culturally oriented. Such a need for oral competence might have started on the Chinese mainland but was further enhanced in Hong Kong mediated by the presence of social learning opportunities, in particular academic learning in the medium of English at the university. Consequently, many participants had much more diversified learning discourses that they could draw on to mobilize their learning efforts.

The disappearance of compulsory high-stakes examinations such as the National College Entrance Examination after arrival in Hong Kong also made it possible for the participants to act according to their preferences. On the Chinese mainland, they were obliged to associate their strategy use with examination success, although many participants were critical of such a learning approach. In Hong Kong, it became possible for them to choose strategies in accordance with their own learning beliefs. Some participants chose strategies that appeared to be more in line with a quantitative learning approach (Benson & Lor, 1999) as a result of their prior learning experiences, but a few participants chose strategies revealing a qualitative conception of learning. The inquiry also identified some continuity in the participants' strategy use, that is their use of memorization strategies for high-stakes examinations, but these strategies were their own choices, however critical these participants used to be of them on the Chinese mainland. They did not claim that they were 'forced' to use these strategies. Instead, their use of these strategies reveals their understanding of their own needs and the absence of some external mediation sources similar to high-stakes examinations, which used to sustain their strategic learning efforts on the Chinese mainland. Therefore, the decision to use high-stakes examinations was an informed choice and was also an attempt to change learning conditions, indicative of the participants' capacity to interpret contextual conditions and make strategy decisions. Moreover, although most participants reported having difficulty in accessing social learning resources, some participants (e.g. Liu and Zhixuan, for more details see Chapter 6) were able to utilize social learning resources to support their language learning efforts. Their accounts of language learning suggest that they made strategic moves to create and maintain social learning networks, which will be examined in detail in Chapter 6. However, the fact that only a few participants managed to have sustainable social learning networks speaks for the contextual constraints on their language learning efforts in Hong Kong.

Contextual Mediation

The data show that most participants were nevertheless constrained in their strategy choices in Hong Kong, although they were more likely to act according to their beliefs and motives in learning English. The disappearance of compulsory high-stakes examinations might have meant more freedom in their choices of strategies in learning English, but it also meant that there were no curricular and examination requirements guiding the participants' strategy use in Hong Kong. In addition, the participants' desire to be academically successful was even stronger as this had become the most viable way for them to achieve the objectives of their educational investment. Ironically, this made them prone to pressure from academic studies, which was quite disruptive to their efforts to learn English. In the worst cases, academic studies made it almost impossible for the participants to regularly devote time to improving English even though they needed effective and persistent efforts to achieve satisfactory language learning.

After arrival in Hong Kong, a few participants, including Liu, Zhixuan and Luonan, supported by the contextual social learning resources (peers) to acquire English, experienced positive reinforcement of cultural learning discourses or dramatic changes in their attitudes and motivation in learning English, leading to changes in their strategy use as well. However, most participants, like Yu and Mengshi (for details see Chapter 6), failed to create and maintain social learning networks supporting their language learning efforts. While seven participants saw English competence related to their self-identities or self-assertion, they found that extra efforts were required to have opportunities to assert themselves meaningfully in English. Even though they made such efforts to socialize with local students, some of them (e.g. Jing) found that they had different social and cultural experiences from those of their local counterparts (Ho *et al.*, 2003; Schack & Schack, 2005), which constituted a significant gap, thus discouraging their use of social learning strategies with local students. As a result, the participants might have been mediated to either use strategies involving little social interaction, such as memorization and watching English TV, or work with other mainland Chinese students for exam-oriented learning.

Conclusion

This chapter has reviewed the reasons as to why the study participants came to Hong Kong for tertiary studies and what they expected of Hong

Kong, and has explored their language learning experiences and strategy use in Hong Kong. It has revealed that the participants' strategy use continued shifting towards being less exam-oriented. While the data indicate that their strategy use exposed the participants to more language input, they reveal mixed findings on the use of social strategies and different experiences of interacting with peers in the language learning process. After arrival in Hong Kong, the inquiry identified shifting discourses about learning English among the participants underlying shifting strategy use, facilitated by their new learning experiences, such as their exposure to the rich English learning resources at the university, including the opportunities to interact with English-competent peers and access many material resources. However, the participants' efforts to learn English through socialization were discouraged or sometimes frustrated by contextual constraints, including academic studies as well as the sociocultural gap with local students. As a result, some participants were inclined to use high-stakes examinations to regulate their learning efforts and achieve their non-linguistic objectives.

The above-mentioned findings, together with those in Chapter 4, illustrate not only the extent of shifts in the participants' strategy use as a group since their arrival in Hong Kong but also the mediation of learning contexts on their strategy use and underlying processes. Yet there is still a need for some deep understanding about the process of these changes in the participants' strategy use. The study has also identified considerable variations among individual participants' experiences of learning and strategy use in Hong Kong, which need to be elaborated with more insights into the interaction process of agency and contextual conditions among individual participants. The study in Phase 2, a longitudinal follow-up inquiry, was designed to capture individual participants' voices and experiences in the process of changing and adapting their strategy use to the shifting learning contexts. The following chapter moves beyond the abstraction of the language learner and presents four case study participants' learning experiences in Hong Kong. Their accounts, addressing the critical issue of time and biographical experiences in the analytical framework (Figure 2.5), will demonstrate how individual language learners tried to 'reflect upon' and 'seek to alter or reinforce the fitness of the social arrangements they encounter for the realization of their own interests' (Sealey & Carter, 2004: 11) and how such efforts are constrained by contextual conditions. From an approach different from that in Chapters 4 and 5, Chapter 6 will describe shifts in the case study participants' strategy use as well as the underlying interaction of agency and contextual conditions.

Chapter 6
Four Case Studies

The previous chapters have given an overall presentation and interpretation of mainland Chinese undergraduates' strategy use in learning English on the Chinese mainland and in Hong Kong, revealing the extent and ways in which their strategy use shifts as a group. The present chapter focuses on the longitudinal case study participants and their language learning experiences during the follow-up phase (Phase 2, September 2004 to July 2006). This longitudinal follow-up study allowed me to explore the ongoing interaction between agency and contextual conditions as it was happening, providing greater depth and insights into the participants' strategic language learning than those reported in their retrospective accounts.

This study phase initially involved six participants (see Table 6.1). However, at the end of the first year, two participants from the Faculty of Business decided to suspend their participation due to their heavy academic workload. This chapter contains biographical case studies of four learners: Liu, Zhixuan, Yu and Mengshi. Although Zhixuan left Hong Kong for one year of exchange studies in the United States, I had lived with him in the same student hall for a year, experiencing what a mainland Chinese student might experience in the hall. For this reason, I decided to include his case in this chapter. It should be noted that many mainland Chinese undergraduates went for exchange studies during their stay in the university as overseas opportunities were considered one of the main incentives attracting them to study in Hong Kong. The inclusion of his case was also an effort to represent what mainland Chinese students could possibly experience in terms of language learning.

Table 6.1 List of the participants and data collection in the longitudinal follow-up phase

Items/name	Mengshi	Yu	Liu	Zhixuan	Rachel	Jingwei
Faculty	Business	Architecture	Business	Science	Business	Business
Gender	M	F	F	M	F	F
Length of participation	2 years	2 years	2 years	1+ year	1 year	1 year
Biographical interviews	Yes	Yes	Yes	Yes	Yes	Yes
Regular conversations	Yes, once a week in term time	Yes, once a week in term time	Yes, once a week in term time	Yes, once a month	Yes, once every two weeks	Yes, once every two weeks
Strategy checklists	Two times, plus exit questionnaire	Two times, plus exit questionnaire	Two times, plus exit questionnaire	Two times, plus exit questionnaire	Two times, plus exit questionnaire	Two times, plus exit questionnaire
Campus observation	Yes, plus hall visits	Yes	Yes	Yes, plus hall visits	Yes	Yes
Classroom observation	Yes, three times	No	Yes, three times	No	Yes, three times	Yes, three times
Email exchanges	Yes	Yes	Yes	Yes	Yes	Yes
Online blogs	No	No	Yes	No	Yes	Yes
Sample works	Yes	Yes	Yes	Yes	Yes	Yes
Member checking	Yes	Yes	Yes	Yes	Yes	Yes

The Longitudinal Follow-Up Study (September 2004 to July 2006)

The longitudinal study (Phase 2) aimed to obtain a wealth of data and an understanding of individual case study participants' language learning experiences and strategic learning efforts after arrival in Hong Kong. Through an extended engagement with the participants, I intended to obtain a 'thick description' and holistic understanding of the phenomenon under research (Geertz, 1973, also Skyrme, 2007). As documented in Table 6.1, a number of elicitation and observation methods, including interviews, observation and strategy use checklists, were used to obtain a multi-perspective understanding of the accounts of the participants' shifting strategy use, which potentially illuminate the interaction of agency and context in their language learning. In particular, in order to retain longitudinal research participants, I intended regular unstructured conversations to be both an instrument to collect the participants' learning experiences and an extra means for the participants to practise English. So, except for Zhixuan, with whom I lived in the same hall, the regular conversations were in English unless they chose to have them in Putonghua. It emerged that these English conversations actually became one of the few opportunities for the participants to engage in meaningful English conversations on a regular basis, which subsequently became a motive for three participants to continue their participation in the research process.

All these casual conversations were audio recorded for summarizing and/or transcription. The recording quickly became a routine for both the participants and myself and did not have any discernible impact on the research participants. After the recording, I carefully listened to these taped conversations and summarized them in written form. Sections related to the participants' language learning were also transcribed verbatim right away. Data analysis began as soon as the data collection started in this study. As I went along with meeting them regularly, I read the gradually accumulating interview transcripts, conversation summaries, research journal entries, emails and other available data related to individual participants at hand to establish a global understanding of these participants. With this global understanding, I critically examined all these data to address the following questions:

(1) What are the major incidents or themes reported by the participants in these accounts?
(2) Are these incidents or themes related to the participants' strategy use or not?

(3) If they are related to the participants' strategy use, do they have a negative or positive impact on their strategy use? And, if so, how?
(4) What are the participants' responses after these incidents?
(5) What do these incidents reveal about the context?

In the process, particular attention was paid to examining how the case study participants' strategy use and learning discourses evolved as they interacted with peers, utilized material conditions and coped with academic studies. I also tried to identify important incidents and recurring themes in the data and made subsequent meetings as venues for further clarification from the participants. Such an ongoing process of analysis and negotiation has led to drafts of research accounts that encapsulated the participants' language learning experiences at the university. I also sent these drafts to the participants for confirmation and arranged to exchange our views concerning these narratives during our subsequent conversations and special meetings. During these meetings, they not only read these draft experiential narratives but also worked together with me to confirm the major themes in their biographical learning experiences in Hong Kong.

It was through such a collaborative research process that the case study narratives, each consisting of a biographical vignette and a thematized biographical narrative, were written, clarified and, to some extent, co-constructed by the research participants and me. Because of such an interpretative process, the case studies appear to be built on periodic conversation data, although their writing was also informed by data from many other sources. All the conversation extracts in this chapter are English originals unless otherwise stated.

Liu

Liu was born into a middle-class family in Fujian Province. Her parents were highly educated and well-respected professionals and were closely involved in her educational progress and language learning. Throughout her academic studies on the Chinese mainland, her family not only provided her with learning resources but also advised her on academic choices and language learning. For instance, her father read many publications related to language learning and helped her to become a good English learner. Her mother had a decisive influence in encouraging her to study in Hong Kong. Liu herself also displayed a strong desire to be successful. During her preparatory year on the Chinese mainland, she started using various strategies to improve her listening and speaking.

She was pleased to find that her English was actually better than that of many others and even better than that of some of the English teachers at the university on the Chinese mainland. Her superb English changed other students' perception that those students who went to study abroad were those who were not intelligent enough to go to the best universities on the Chinese mainland. Therefore, she found that her English was critical to her self-perception as an 'elite' student on the Chinese mainland. She was also determined to be an 'elite' student in Hong Kong although, for various reasons, she was not accepted by the university as a scholarship student.

Liu's two years' language learning experiences in Hong Kong were intertwined with her persistent search for more learning opportunities and regular setbacks frustrating her strategic moves. She had apparently managed her integration with local students quite well, which helped create a facilitative learning environment for her learning of English and Cantonese. At the same time, a gradual process of psychological distancing from local students can also be seen in her experiential accounts, as she progressively moved closer to the mainland Chinese students' community and was socialized into different patterns of strategy use. The selected biographical episodes are intended to illustrate these contradictory processes and reveal the interplay between Liu's agency and the context underlying her strategy use.

Manipulating contextual resources for learning English

The data indicate that Liu, like other participants in the study, believed that the university provided a better English language learning environment than institutions on the Chinese mainland. For this reason, she felt that her strategy use in learning English was greatly facilitated by the new environment. The university attracts many international students and local students with high English proficiency. It also recruits high-calibre mainland Chinese students whose English is likely to be more proficient than their counterparts on the Chinese mainland. In other words, there were many material resources and proficient English users (social resources) available to support Liu's English language learning. Our regular conversation summaries show that, starting from her arrival in Hong Kong, Liu had been actively using these resources to improve her English as well as her Cantonese. In the case of learning English, the comparison of two strategy use checklists completed by her in the first and second semesters reveals that she progressively adopted a greater variety of strategic behaviour to increase her exposure to English and to use English in Hong Kong.

In her first semester at the university, she regularly listened to English radio or watched English TV programmes; she also established an English-speaking partnership with another mainland Chinese student; she tried to implement a rule to ensure that she would use English for all academic matters including discussions and tutorials, where students easily lapsed into Cantonese and even Putonghua. Apart from these strategic moves, she invested her time and energy in making friends and socializing with local students in her hall and in her faculty, which contributed to her expanded access to local students' groups and Cantonese competence and helped increase her social opportunities for using English. Far more importantly, it gave her a sense of belonging to the student community. In the following interview extract, she describes how she started a language-exchange partnership with a local student, which evolved into a scheme involving three languages:

> One day, I got a message from an Arts student, a girl. She said that she was interested in learning Putonghua. She asked me whether I was interested in language exchange with her. At that time, my Cantonese was poor. So I agreed. For the first time meeting, both of us talked in Putonghua because I could not express myself in Cantonese. Last night, both of us were speaking in Cantonese (laughter). Do you think it funny? Hong Kong people could not change their human nature. Whenever they could speak Cantonese, they would speak Cantonese. Because her Putonghua was not too good, sometimes she would use a lot of English to explain herself. Once she started speaking English to me, I would switch to English. But when she switched back to Putonghua, I would try to speak in Cantonese. If I failed in my attempt, I would use Putonghua. It was just like that. In the beginning, I would ask her about basic terms in Cantonese. In the middle, we spoke more English because she found my English was good. So she was inter-ested in practising English with me. In the end, both of us switched to Cantonese. I think that it is funny. They could not change their human nature of speaking Cantonese. (3 September 2004)

The episode sheds light on Liu's readiness to embrace every possible lan-guage learning opportunity arising from her exchanges with local stu-dents. It also reveals the linguistic complexity that Liu had to cope with to maximize the development of her Cantonese and English competence. As she skillfully manoeuvred the language exchange scheme to benefit her Cantonese and English learning, she also had to avoid a common phe-nomenon shared by many mainland Chinese students, namely their opportunities to use English significantly decreased when they were identified as able speakers of Cantonese. Therefore, it became a strategic move for Liu to use the evolving relationships among three languages (Cantonese, English and Putonghua) in the wider social context for her own benefit. Such strategic efforts revealed her agency in taking control of her own language learning and participating in the student community (Norton & Toohey, 2001), but the mediation of linguistic complexity in the learning context is also manifested in her account.

Challenges in utilizing social learning resources

In spite of Liu's active strategy use to carve out a favourable niche for her language learning, the complicated learning context constrained her strategy use in acquiring linguistic competence and striving for her acceptance in the learning community. Although the early conversation summaries indicate that her integration into the students' community was quite successful, the data recorded a process of alienation from local students in her experiences, in which she felt that the differences she had with them gradually became more, not less, apparent in ongoing social exchanges. Consequently, she felt that she was prevented from participating fully in student community life.

It is characteristic of many highly motivated mainland Chinese students in Hong Kong that they are always anxious to prove themselves competent members of the community. One way for them to achieve this is, in addition to having good academic results, to participate in numerous student competitions. In two years, Liu made a few unsuccessful attempts to participate in student competitions. The particular student competition in this episode, a student proposal competition, which took place three months after her arrival, also functioned as an incentive for her to practise English intensively as the competition was organized by a local branch of an international student organization. However, according to Liu, on the first-round proposal-making day, she disappointedly found that Cantonese was the dominant language, in spite of the international profile claimed by the competition organizers, because most participants were local students. The competition process gave rise to the first significant clash recorded in the data between Liu and the local students. The competition required all the participants to work in a group and discuss the assigned reading materials for making proposals. Liu intended to make a proposal that somehow linked the Chinese mainland and Hong Kong, but local participants were more interested in proposing topics like corporate responsibility, to which she attached little significance. In the end, when the group voted for the proposal to be adopted, her proposal was turned down; it only obtained three votes from mainland Chinese participants, including herself, and no local participants supported her proposal. This result was certainly disappointing for Liu but the implications were even more serious. The rejection, along with daily experiences of 'us–other' differentiation in the media and social exchanges (Ho *et al.*, 2003; Li *et al.*, 1995; Ma & Fung, 1999; Schack & Schack, 2005), made her suspect that her proposal was not treated fairly because it was about the Chinese mainland:

> I would like to talk about mainland [. . .]. It created problems for me because sometimes I had to be judged by a group of local students. They would think you odd, very odd, talk differently. When their culture and values are not there, they think that you are not one of them. [. . .] Maybe, we have different concerns and cultural values. I feel that I am not one of them. Maybe in the very beginning, I felt that I was lucky that I am not one of them because I have different opinions. I think that I may help them to change, well, show them that there are different ways of thinking. But now I feel that I could not no matter how hard I tried because it was too difficult. (15 November 2004)

This incident, together with others, left Liu with the impression that she could speak but was constantly not heard in the student community. It was from such socialization experiences that she discovered the insurmountable 'wall' between her and the community and the difficulty in securing a role in the local community. She realized that there were more than linguistic barriers for her to overcome in Hong Kong; the cultural gap also prevented her from becoming a fully participatory member in the students' community, regardless of her shared cultural heritage and ethnic background with local students. After the competition, she did not give up her use of social strategies with local students to improve her English and Cantonese entirely. However, the data do show that the incident had a negative impact on her sense of belonging to the community and use of social strategies in language learning. In previous conversations, she had already complained that her insistence on using English alone put her at risk of being distanced by other Putonghua-speaking mainland Chinese students, leading to occasional feelings of isolation. After this incident, she mentioned more frequently her mainland Chinese friends in her conversations and eventually after six months in Hong Kong, she found herself using more Putonghua and less Cantonese and English:

> I speak more and more Putonghua now. Now if some people approach, Hong Kong people, I will speak Putonghua to them sometimes. I will

not speak Cantonese to them. I do not know why. Even my professor hands me a handout, I will say 'xiexie' (Thank you) even though I know how to speak Cantonese. (9 March 2005)

As she started appreciating the fact that she shared more with other mainland Chinese students, her strategy use in learning English began to display more influences from mainland Chinese peers.

Regaining power in learning English

Although her unsatisfactory participation experiences in the student community discouraged her active use of social learning strategies, the data reveal that Liu attempted to regain momentum in learning English by expanding her vocabulary after she found herself using more Putonghua and less English. As she spent time interacting with her mainland Chinese peers, she found that she was exposed to a popular discourse among them, which views achieving high academic results, receiving a doctoral scholarship from an American university or getting a job offer from a prestigious company in Hong Kong as the pinnacle of success for a mainland Chinese student at the university. She saw that many of her mainland Chinese friends were motivated by such visions to endure a stressful process of memorizing the Graduate Record Exam (GRE) vocabulary list in preparation for the GRE exam, a gatekeeper examination for those who wish to apply for graduate studies in North American universities. She also noted that many other mainland Chinese students felt obliged to do so without actually believing in its long-term impact on their acquisition of linguistic competence. Usually these students tried to memorize three sub-lists of new words in the vocabulary list and review all the sub-lists they had memorized earlier every day until they had reviewed the same word 7 times. The most popular vocabulary book had 51 sub-lists (6000 commonly tested words in total) and in theory took 17 days of concentrated effort to memorize. This was a daunting task for many. Nevertheless, Liu found it necessary to spend time memorizing and reviewing the GRE wordlists to acquire more vocabulary. As she once detested rote memorization and systematic reviewing of vocabulary, she modified the popular memorization approach to suit her needs:

I could not do it myself. It was terrible. But I decided to review two lists a week, after a semester, I can finish forty lists. From the beginning of the semester, I have completed 8 lists. It is not that bad. The problem is whether I will persist. I think that my way is much better. Because in the 17-days way, people just look at or stare at the words, they do not know how to read, they do not know how to use them. They do not care. (21 September 2005)

While her decision to memorize GRE wordlists was mediated by her mainland Chinese peers, the data suggest that she understood the importance of having a large vocabulary and was aware of the necessity of having her own reasons for this memorization effort. Otherwise, she felt that it was extremely difficult for her to continue memorizing words. However, she could not find meanings and discourses that could motivate her learning efforts among her mainland Chinese peers. Many of her peers started spending time memorizing words because of the uncertainties upon graduation that they foresaw. Although these students initially intended to seek employment in Hong Kong, they began to seriously consider preparing for plan B, that is, undertaking postgraduate studies elsewhere as the linguistic and sociocultural differences they had with local students added to their insecurity and uncertainty as a result of being non-locals in Hong Kong. In addition, there were also some mainland Chinese students who regarded Hong Kong's English-medium tertiary education as a stepping stone for them to pursue postgraduate studies in countries like the United States and Great Britain. Although Liu probably shared some of these motives, she did not find the images of successful graduates in the dominant discourses among her mainland peers inspiring. In other words, she wanted to have her own voice in learning English and sought to be different:

> There is always a voice inside me, telling me to come back to China. But after I came to Hong Kong, everybody is talking about going abroad, going overseas, PhD, finding a good job, staying in Hong Kong, making a lot of money. My own voice is becoming less and less audible. I cannot say it. I need to have my own voice. [...] Now because I found studying English, if you have some good knowledge of English, it really means something, [...] if I have a good knowledge of English, if I go back, it is OK just for me to be an English teacher, it does not matter. [...] Even if I do not have to be a PHD, I can still help other people. (21 September 2005)

In a series of conversations, she recounted how she found new meanings in learning English after becoming a fan of a nationwide *Super Girl* competition winner in the summer of 2005. The *Super Girl* competition is like a Chinese version of *American Idol* except that all the contestants are female (Jacks, 2005; Keane, 2006). The winner in 2005 was an unusual cultural icon elected by millions of young Chinese through text messaging, who possesses 'attitude, originality and a proud androgyny that defied Chinese norms' (Jacks, 2005). The message conveyed through this cultural icon to her as well as to thousands of fans was clear, that is, it is wonderful to be different:

> Maybe in the bottom of my heart, I feel that I was a little bit like Li Yu Chun, when I was in high school. If I did something like her, it would be perfect. If I was a Li Yu Chun, [...] I will not do what I am doing now. I am not dreaming a star life. Now she is a superstar. But before that, she was just a common girl like everybody. A common girl. But I did not choose to be like her. I focused on my academic studies instead. (21 September 2005)

As Liu found that her idol could not pronounce English words properly in the contest, she decided to write a letter telling her how to pronounce them properly. In return, she received a photo with her idol's signature. An apparently insignificant incident empowered her with her own voice in learning English as she became aware that her English competence could be truly meaningful to her even if she returned to the Chinese mainland. As a result, she realized that learning English could have many other meanings and she did not have to define its meaning as something like receiving a good job offer in Hong Kong or doing doctoral studies in the United States, as did many mainland Chinese students.

Such reflections gave her a sense of ownership in her language learning, which made memorization efforts much more pleasant and enjoyable for her. The whole episode showed that Liu, as a social agent, could reflexively and purposefully transform a series of strenuous efforts into something meaningful in her pursuit of linguistic competence, by drawing inspiration from her own life experiences. However, this does not negate the possibility that Liu adopted memorization strategies because she was almost obliged to do so by peers from her social group and the situation she found herself in after discovering the enduring gap between local students and herself. Thus, her strategy use was a product of the interplay between her agency and contextual realities, both having mediated her language learning and strategy use.

Zhixuan

Zhixuan grew up in a family that had strong links with the educated 'elite' in Beijing. His uncle and aunt, both having been visiting scholars to top American universities, had a deep influence on his attraction to the United States and his motivation for learning English. He admitted that he was 'Americanized' before he even came to Hong Kong, believing that

'American culture is the best'. He had been pursuing his dream of going to the States for years. In high school, he was obliged to work hard for English examinations although he knew that exam-oriented learning did not help improve his English. During the preparatory year on the Chinese mainland, he had been actively working on his English, in particular his speaking and listening. He also sought to expand his understanding of America, taking courses in American culture. However, it was not until he came to Hong Kong and attended a summer camp organized by a group of American university students that he began to have his first real communication experience with American students. As a northern Chinese, he knew that it would not be easy for him to pick up a good command of Cantonese, so he decided to give it up and devote his time to learning only English while he was in Hong Kong as a science student.

The accounts of Zhixuan show that the complexity of the language learning task in Hong Kong could be reduced significantly as he considered his stay in Hong Kong transitory and had a well-designed plan to go to the United States for further studies upon graduation. As an extremely motivated English language learner, he was ready to seize all possible learning opportunities in Hong Kong. He was also a focused learner, spending most of his time and energy on academic studies and English. Moreover, the differences that mainland Chinese students had with local students had little influence on Zhixuan's language learning experiences. Because of his decision related to further studies, he actively utilized contextual resources to support his own language learning efforts. Zhixuan socialized mainly with exchange students, particularly those from the States and had little to do with local and other mainland Chinese students. He also spent a year in the States for exchange studies where he further refined his English. The thematized accounts in the following sections illustrate how he made full use of English learning opportunities in Hong Kong in preparation for his exchange year and improved his English during his stay in the United States.

Utilize learning resources

Zhixuan's first reported satisfactory English language learning experience took place when he arrived in Hong Kong to attend a Summer English Camp organized by the China Affairs Office of the university in the summer of 2004. It was an immersion style camp for English learners, where a group of American college students acted as tutors. In the English camp, Zhixuan experienced using English intensively for social communication, which encouraged him to put great effort into improving his listening comprehension and oral competence, as he considered himself 'probably the weakest among all the scholarship students' in English at that time. When the camp was over, he believed that he had made some significant progress in speaking and he made good friends with American tutors at the camp. In the camp, his understanding of American culture, in particular his knowledge of American classics such as De Tocqueville's work, must have impressed his American counterparts deeply. His interest in Christianity and his belief in Christianity as an integral part of American culture might have also made it easier for him to establish a close relationship with the American tutors, all of whom were evangelical Christians. Moreover, his reflectivity and readiness to seize any appropriate learning opportunities also had a lasting impact on his strategy use. However, he was not likely to adopt certain learning methods or strategies simply based on other people's advice. Instead, he would often search from his relevant life experiences to identify the most appropriate ways of learning. As an example, he recalled how he sought advice on memorizing classical texts from his American teachers to strengthen his belief in the importance of memorization in his learning of English:

> It is important for a language learner to memorize when learning his or her mother tongue. It is also important for me to memorize certain English texts. But I cannot memorize everything. That is why I need to do some research to know what should be memorized. I also asked my American teachers this. I asked them whether they had memorized any texts when they were in primary and secondary schools in the States. They said that they had memorized something. So I asked them to send them to me through emails, I mean, the titles of their memorized texts. So I can have a list of texts (for memorization). I tried to learn English as if I was learning Chinese, as if I was learning my mother tongue. (25 August 2004, translated from Chinese)

Zhixuan's immersion experience in the summer English camp had provided him with an opportunity to compare his previous experience of learning Chinese, his mother tongue, to his current experience of learning English. The necessity of memorizing classical texts was a useful strategy in his perception as he reflected on his previous experiences. The importance of using a dictionary in extensive reading was another conclusion he inferred from his past experience of reading difficult Chinese magazines:

> In the camp, I tried to recall how I learnt Chinese. Then I remembered that I had a very difficult time reading a magazine a long time ago (when I was very small). There were so many words I did not understand at

that time. So I had to rely on the dictionary to go on reading it until I became unwilling to use the dictionary. I spent hour after hour reading a magazine [...] at that time, it was regarded as unfit for my age. I am not saying that it was something immoral. It was just too difficult to read. (25 August 2004, translated from Chinese)

The reflection on his difficulties in reading Chinese encouraged him to read English books although they might contain some words beyond his level of English. He mentioned that he had started to like reading English books to improve his linguistic competence in English:

Now I have also become fond of reading books. I had already begun to read English books, mainly to improve my English and my vocabulary. (25 August 2004, translated from Chinese)

In the account given above, the participant appeared to be a highly self-regulated language learner who drew on his previous language learning experiences to inform his current pursuit of English competence. Such reflections and regulatory efforts on language learning revealed the participant's agency in learning English in a context that might appear to be constraining for other study participants. Highly motivated, he used to spend time memorizing English texts and looking up all the new words he encountered in reading.

The challenge of sustaining a space for learning English

In this inquiry, Zhixuan was one of the most successful participants to integrate learning English with academic learning through English. In one of our conversations, he recounted how he had been utilizing academic studies to create opportunities for learning English, not only to expand his vocabulary, but also to have more oral practice, especially during his first semester in Hong Kong. His decision not to learn any Cantonese probably facilitated his efforts to concentrate his energy on learning English. During the first few weeks, while his mainland counterparts were busy with participating in all sorts of orientation camps organized by their student societies and residential halls, he benefited from the exemption from such orientation activities and devoted the time to watching videos and listening to the English radio to improve his listening comprehension. He also regularly spent some time reading English news and watching English news programmes:

In Hong Kong, I mainly focused on reading and writing because they were very useful. At that time, I could only finish one page in one hour. It was too much. It was really painful. [...] whenever I met an unknown word, I would look it up. It was hard. In the beginning, [...] I spent much more time on learning English than I planned. [...] For about three months in August, September and October, I just focused on learning English. I got up early and went to sleep late. I worked very hard. (27 July 2006, translated from Chinese)

In addition, he spent most of the learning time reading his textbooks carefully as he tried his best to adopt a balanced approach to his academic studies and learning of English, focusing on reading English materials related to the field of his academic studies. Through such intensive learning efforts, he acquired both specialist and linguistic knowledge. However, as he understood that he had limited time for a wide range of skills and competences, he focused on learning what was essential to him and was not willing to move beyond the boundary of his own disciplinary learning. If he had to take some extra courses as required by the university, he often chose courses that helped him to learn more English or American culture. His comment on course selection reveals his desire to economize his efforts for maximum benefits in both academic studies and learning English:

Although I did read some other materials for other courses because I chose some courses in Hong Kong, I mean, those not in my academic major studies. I had taken a literature course [...] if I did not have to take it, then I would not choose it. If I had to take some non-major courses, I would probably choose this course because I was more interested in the course than other courses. (27 July 2006, translated from Chinese)

While Zhixuan economized his efforts to expand his English vocabulary through reading his course materials with great care, he took advantage of collaborative learning at the department, which required him and other students to spend a lot of time together constructing and developing their subject knowledge, for instance, having small group discussions. He used his advanced understanding of chemistry to have academic discussions in English with a group of students who were proficient in English so that he could have more opportunities to use English. Like Liu, he was also good at establishing social networks to facilitate his learning efforts:

I made a few friends with my department because we have work to do together. Well, I mean that we can discuss chemistry. [...] I have a lot of interaction with my classmates but not with my hall mates. Of course, they talk in English. Some people will try to get something from me [...] because I know a lot of chemistry terms in Chinese [...].

I learnt all my chemistry in China in Chinese. (7 February 2005, translated from Chinese)

This also explains why Zhixuan did not want to interact much with his peers in the same hall. Firstly, he had no shared medium of communication with them since he had been determined not to learn Cantonese. Secondly, there was no reason for communication for they had no shared interest. Consequently, he avoided many difficult issues faced by other participants in the study who felt obliged to learn Cantonese and integrate into the student community. Instead, Zhixuan spent most of the socialization time interacting with international students:

I just sleep in my hall and spend most of my time outside of my hall, either in the library or classrooms. I seldom talk to my floor mates. They can only speak Cantonese. And they are too shy to speak Putonghua. But I have a good relationship with my neighbours. One is from Australia and the other is from Denmark. And also Lilly, a friend I met in the American Youth Culture course. She is an American. (7 February 2005, translated from Chinese)

However, the desire to have a good academic record and a mastery of English undermined his quality of life. After his return from exchange studies in the United States, he saw his life in the United States as being much happier because he had not had much social life and many friends in Hong Kong. As I examined his early accounts of academic life in Hong Kong, the contextual conditions did seem to have made his life more stressful although this was the result of his own choice. In other words, even though the data show that he could manage his language learning successfully in Hong Kong, he still suffered from social isolation as a mainland Chinese student committed to academic studies and learning English. In the end, his efforts did pay off since he achieved a high level of English and became fully prepared for his exchange study in the United States. In fact, Zhixuan felt that, among all the international exchange students his host university in the United States received during the year, he considered himself the best in terms of English proficiency. He had indeed learnt English in Hong Kong to a level that he could fully communicate in it during his stay in the United States.

An American experience

Zhixuan appreciated the fact that Hong Kong had prepared him linguistically for his exchange study in the United States. Without a year of

learning English in Hong Kong, he believed that it would have been quite
difficult for him to adjust to academic studies and daily life in the United
States. As a result, when he went to the United States, he no longer felt
the need to learn English. The data confirm that he did not put any special effort into learning English because opportunities to learn and use
English were so abundant that he did not need to make an effort to create
opportunities for use as he did in Hong Kong. In addition, he admitted
that he did not have to be fully 'conscious' of the learning process and
regulate the content he learnt in order that he could learn perfect English:

> I did not learn English in the States. [...] There are some differences
> between Hong Kong and the States. I was not worried in the States. I
> was worried in Hong Kong because all people here speak English
> with accents. So I had to be *conscious* [my italics] about what I needed
> to learn and what I should not learn. I needed to make sure whether
> the way that a word was used in Hong Kong was proper. [...] in the
> States, I mainly socialized with Americans and I had no such need to
> be on the alert. I did not have to think about this question all the time.
> It was relaxing for me. And I learnt English faster. (27 July 2006, trans-
> lated from Chinese)

The most important means for him to improve his English in the United
States was to socialize with his fellow American students and other inter-
national students in English. He found that the host university was truly
international and American students were willing to receive outsiders.
Consequently, he did not feel that he was a foreigner at all on the campus.
Through regular interaction with other students and friends in English, he
not only felt that he was much happier in the United States than in Hong
Kong but he also managed to make some significant progress in his
English. In particular, he noticed that his accent had improved:

> I had been trying my best to change my accent. [...] There was a class-
> mate, with whom I always talked in the first semester, who told me
> that I had a strong Chinese accent. Later he told me that he could not
> detect my Chinese accent. [...] My host family also told me that it was
> sometimes difficult to understand me when I first went there. I did not
> realize that I had such a strong accent. But now, I may not be perfect
> but my host family friends have no problems in understanding me.
> (27 July 2006, translated from Chinese)

In the United States, his academic studies and socialization took most of
his time. As a result, he no longer had time for watching TV and reading
English news as he used to do in Hong Kong. His decreased interest in
news was partly related to the fact that he had little opportunity to discuss

political issues with his friends. Consequently, he had no use for the language and knowledge acquired through reading news. Therefore, he felt the time spent on reading and watching news had to be reduced:

> Later on, we did not talk about politics. Most of the online news was political news. [...] I was not particularly interested in it. [...] we often talked about science and then our countries because I was talking with other international students. And with my lab mates, about academic problems. (27 July 2006, translated from Chinese)

Among the friends he made in the United States, many were actually international exchange students like him, including some German and Japanese friends. There was an Asian American student who had a close relationship with him. He also mentioned that he had developed a congenial relationship with an old professor in his department. Apparently, Zhixuan had been one of the lucky students who had integrated well into the student community, or particular student groups he found on the university campus. He was either placed in a social circle or, by accident, he was one of the founding members of a particular social circle. For instance, the social circle in the laboratory where he worked as an undergraduate assistant was built on the academic discipline he found himself in. This circle provided opportunities for him to improve his spoken English through socialization.

Like many other participants in this study, Zhixuan identified himself as one of the academic 'elite'. To maintain his position among the social 'elite', he was determined to pursue postgraduate studies in the United States upon his graduation in Hong Kong. For this reason, he had to take the GRE test for which dozens of his mainland Chinese counterparts in Hong Kong had been preparing. At one time, he tried to read through a book given by a professor as an award for his academic performance in his course, hoping that the reading would help him to prepare for the test. As he realized that it was too time-consuming to go through the book, checking every unknown word, he decided to give it up. Instead, he resorted to doing what many other Chinese mainland students did, namely memorizing the GRE wordlists intensively:

> I was particularly busy in the second semester. And there was also GRE. I wanted to memorize the words (I encountered in the book) to prepare for GRE. But later, I found that it was more efficient to memorize the GRE wordlists. I knew that I would forget a lot of words I had memorized. But I did not have time. Time was short. (27 July 2006, translated from Chinese)

However, unlike many other study participants, he saw English as his 'primary language' and imagined himself as a member of the academic 'elite' circle he had found in the United States. Among all the study participants, he was one of the few learners who articulated such clear integrative motives for learning English. He was one of the few students who could shut himself off from the outside reality and maintain a favourable setting that would help him to reach his goals of academic elitism and English competence. Zhixuan's experiences indicate that language learners are likely to sustain a social space for language learning and strategy use, provided that they have a strong commitment to their learning goals, an understanding of the language learning context and appropriate skills in manipulating these conditions. His accounts are also suggestive of the importance of his exercises of agency, his will and capacity (power) to act otherwise (Giddens, 1976, 1984), in his pursuit of linguistic competence, although one can also detect the constraints imposed by contextual conditions upon him.

Yu

Yu grew up in a middle-class professional family on the Chinese mainland, with parents who were not only interested in her educational progress but also anxiously engaged in her language learning. Her parents put great effort into supervising her learning of English and forced her to memorize as many English words as possible when she was a young child. Although her attitude towards memorization was quite negative because of this experience, she found that her English exam results had always been among the best in her class. After her parents decided that she should go to Hong Kong for tertiary studies, she found that she desperately needed to improve her spoken English. She was not satisfied with the English instruction in her university during the preparatory year on the Chinese mainland. Together with other Hong Kong-bound students, she employed a tutor to help her to improve her English.

The data reveal the enormous challenges that Yu encountered in coping with the demands placed on her to learn Cantonese and English and to pursue academic studies in Hong Kong. All of these were competing for her precious time and in turn were becoming major themes of her language learning experiences in Hong Kong. On the one hand, she needed to improve her Cantonese so that she could participate in the learning community effectively. On the other hand, she appreciated the paramount importance of English in the current study in the English medium and in future workplaces. Since her academic studies often prevented her from investing more time and energy in learning English, like many other mainland Chinese students, she struggled to improve her English. Eventually, this struggle culminated in her decision to prepare for the GRE test even though she was still unsure as to whether she would go to North America for graduate studies or not. The following descriptions taken from the longitudinal inquiry highlight the constraints in her language learning environments and her frustrated language learning efforts.

Learning Cantonese

In comparison with other mainland Chinese students, Yu's strategy use in learning English was probably most mediated by the collaborative learning approach in her Faculty, where the dominant socialization medium was Cantonese. As an architecture student, apart from attending lectures, she spent most of her time on design work in the studio with all the other students from the same cohort. In the first semester, she collaborated with a local student in working on a 1:1 model designed according to *Butterfly Lovers*, a famous Chinese folk tale. In another semester, groups of 20 students were asked to submit a final project, with each group further divided into smaller teams, each responsible for a different section of the project. According to tradition, Yu was asked to be a helper for senior students and took junior students as helpers when she became a second-year student. The strong emphasis on collective teamwork and the collaborative learning environment required a common language for students to share their understanding and knowledge with each other, a decision beyond the control of Yu and even the official English medium instruction policy in the university. The dominant language for peer interaction was Cantonese even though many of Yu's local group mates were international school graduates and non-JUPAS (Joint University Programmes Admission System) students who were highly proficient in English. Thus, the studio generated a pressing necessity for her to reach at least a functional level of Cantonese:

> I try to communicate with my classmates in Cantonese because local students, after all, like to use Cantonese. If I use Putonghua or English, it will cause barriers in our exchanges. They will not be too willing to talk to me. If I use Putonghua, Putonghua will be too difficult for them. (28 September 2004)

> If I keep speaking Putonghua, maybe they (local students) do not want to speak to me. (Because) They have a lot of chances to speak to other students in Cantonese. So I will have less chance to communicate with others. [...] I speak Putonghua to myself. And I speak Cantonese to my classmates in order to be part of them. (20 November 2004)

Cantonese was not only important in the learning process but also an important asset for her future career. The normal path for an architecture graduate to become a registered architect in Hong Kong requires the graduate to take a one-year traineeship in an architectural firm, which is followed by a two-year master's level study and professional examinations. This meant that she would have to spend quite some time working and studying in Hong Kong before getting her professional qualification. As a result, there was a great need for her to acquire an appropriate command of Cantonese to enable her to function in teamwork with local students at the university and colleagues upon graduation. Apart from this, Cantonese was also the dominant medium for socialization in the residential hall where Yu lived. The residential hall was an even closer social community, in which each resident was expected to acquire a shared hall identity through participating in all sorts of activities. For this reason, she was a member of the hall basketball team for some time. In some sense, the hall was a good place for her as well as many other mainland Chinese students to learn Cantonese:

> I started learning Cantonese in the orientation camp. I just listened to Cantonese all days and all the week in the orientation. In the beginning, I could not understand what they talked about, so somebody translated for me. I participated in it for three days. I could not understand it totally. I still had barriers. After resting for a few days, I suddenly realized that I could understand it much more. I do not know why it was so. (12 December 2004)

However, a functional command of Cantonese did not make life and study much easier for Yu. There were still many obstacles against her full participation in the residential and learning community. For instance, she could not fully express herself and often felt stigmatized when her accent betrayed her true identity as a mainland Chinese student; this would happen whenever a local student switched to Putonghua after talking to her for a while. Although she appreciated that it was probably a gesture of goodwill on the part of the local speaker, she still felt uncomfortable about such sudden changes:

> I do not feel good about it. (Gao: Why?) It was just like this. If I do not speak, they cannot tell me that I am not one of them. They cannot tell that I am actually not from Hong Kong. The sudden change in their ways of talking to me always reminds me of the fact that I am not from Hong Kong. It is an act to differentiate my identity from theirs. I feel annoyed for there is always someone who wants to separate me out from them. (30 May 2006)

This extract reveals her feeling of defeat at discovering the apparent failure in her efforts to learn Cantonese so as to integrate into the local community. Her experiential account also indicates that her integration efforts through Cantonese were not a complete success because of the cultural gaps she had with local students (Ho *et al.*, 2003; Schack & Schack, 2005), in some cases leading to great frustration for her. For instance, differences towards study and life that she had with local students tended to constrain their relationships. As a fee-paying mainland Chinese student, she was much more concerned than her local counterparts with her academic performance and willing to put every effort into her work. Consequently, she found that she had no time for leisure and social activities. Yet her local group members appeared to have a different view:

> [...] their lifestyle is a bit different from mine. They like to sing Karaoke. Sometimes they spend too much time on doing something meaningless. I think that they are wasting time. (20 November 2004)

In addition, there were tensions in the studio. Yu noted that local students tended to play music and chat with each other when working in the studio. Music, conversations and other sounds created distracting noises for her when she felt that she desperately needed to concentrate on her design work in search for inspiration and problem solution. Such tensions gradually built up after students worked for long hours, often several nights in the studio. It was not unusual for local students to have nervous breakdowns and therefore it was understandable for Yu to experience some emotional outbursts, which could put further strains on her relationship with the others. In other words, the collaborative learning at Yu's Faculty, together with the broader sociocultural gaps that she had with local students, somehow undermined her pursuit of linguistic competence in Cantonese and English.

Strategy use in learning English

While Yu tried to integrate into the residential and learning communities through the medium of Cantonese, her struggle with learning English also dominated her language learning experiences in Hong Kong. She apparently saw the efforts in learning Cantonese to be in conflict with her struggles to obtain a better command of English. For this reason, a recurring theme of the conversations with her in the first year was the regret that she had 'been using too much Cantonese and had no opportunities to use English' (4 December 2004, English original). On one occasion, she found herself speaking to a native English tutor in an English language class in Cantonese (28 September 2004). This became a serious problem because she had to defend her own work and contributions before tutors and other group members in English once she finished her design work with her Cantonese-speaking group mates. She understood the critical importance of English as English presentations were important in deciding her final results:

> In fact, English matters more to me than Cantonese. (28 September 2004)

Yu faced a double-edged language learning struggle, in which she had to put extra effort into improving her English and, at the same time, continue working on her Cantonese. Like many other mainland Chinese students, she managed to expand her exposure to English by watching English TV programmes and movies apparently because TV was one of the most accessible sources of English input she could find in Hong Kong. The significance of watching English programmes and movies shifted as her academic studies progressed in Hong Kong. At the beginning, she was apparently motivated to watch English programmes and movies to improve her English, especially after she felt that she had been using too much Cantonese. Later on, it also became one of the major means for her to relax after a full day's study:

> I watch TV in English. When I watch TV, I just want to improve my English. (12 December 2004)

> I went to watch English movies for improving my English and relaxation. (5 February 2005)

> I watch TV, most of the time, English TV, on CCTV, ATV world. I watch David Late Show. [...] CCTV 9 is much easier for me to understand. Maybe because of its accent and the key words they choose. For the other English channels, I have difficulty in understanding them. [...] If I got tired, I would watch TV because I do not need to think too much while watching TV. (3 March 2005)

Moreover, the necessity for her to use English in lectures was a source of pressure and anxiety, stimulating her to put effort into learning English. In the first year, she repeatedly talked about a compelling need to improve her spoken English and the fear inside her when she was speaking English to native speakers, course tutors, English-proficient local students and other strangers. Consequently, at the beginning of her studies, she used her deficiency in Cantonese to seek opportunities to practise English when interacting with her local student partners when collaborating on projects.

Such practices, although limited, had a positive impact on her pursuit of oral English competence:

> I cannot express myself in Cantonese efficiently. So I use English and Cantonese at the same time. (20 November 2004)

> I still made some progress in English, [...] in spoken English. When we (my partner and I) were designing the model, I kept talking English. (18 December 2004)

Unfortunately, once her Cantonese improved, she lost the opportunities to practise English and found herself using more and more Cantonese. Later, she was even alarmed to find herself speaking less Putonghua because her design work had taken up most of her time and drastically reduced her social time. For this particular reason, she persisted in having a weekly conversation in English in this follow-up study as it became almost the only opportunity for her to practise English.

In addition to her speaking problems, at the beginning of her academic studies, she felt that she needed to increase her vocabulary to cope with academic studies conducted in English. Consequently, even though she did not wish to memorize words, she found that she had to do so. Apart from memorizing words from a vocabulary book she brought with her, she tried to memorize words encountered in textbooks and course materials. However, she found that her memorization effort produced disappointing results since she was not able to remember the words that she tried to memorize:

> I really need words helping me to understand other people's English [...] I just have one book on vocabulary and tried to remember words. Every day twenty words or so. Just go through it. Most of them I have already been familiar with. I just take out those difficult ones. [...] I also tried to memorize words from architecture textbooks. (6 November 2004)

> I met many of the words I used to memorize before. But I do not remember them so I had to check them in the dictionary. Even if I go back to the same word many times, I just could not remember its meanings. I just become familiar with the word. But most of the words I used to memorize, I can remember them because I need to use them here. (5 February 2005)

Although Yu reported limited success at improving her English competence, she continued struggling to improve it against all odds, in spite of her stressful academic studies and inability to expand her vocabulary.

A desperate struggle to learn English

Prior to the commencement of the second academic year, she made a final major attempt to improve her English and decided to memorize GRE words like many other mainland Chinese students. The decision to memorize GRE words was mediated by other mainland Chinese students who were planning to embark on further studies abroad, especially in the United States. Yu appeared to have some mixed feelings about her decision. She felt that she would be at a disadvantage if she did not do what others were doing. She was also worried about whether she would be able to secure a trainee opportunity in Hong Kong as the job market for architects had become increasingly competitive. Therefore, it was desirable for her to seek overseas professional qualifications. Apart from these practical concerns and worries, she did have a strong urge to improve her English. For instance, she always tried to improve her English during vacations when she had more time, even though she seldom succeeded in achieving anything in learning English. This time, she hoped that she would manage to attain some tangible learning success by participating in the popular craze for memorizing GRE words:

> One of my classmates (mainland Chinese student) who is from Beijing went to New Oriental School because she wanted to take GRE or TOEFL. She wanted to go abroad after her undergraduate study. I have not decided whether to go or not. But I need to take it as well. [...] I plan to take the course in Beijing in August. I just want to push myself to learn more English. [...] Everybody else is doing the same thing. If I do not do it, I feel that I am losing something. [...] They say that the school is very good at this thing, guessing exam questions. [...] a lot of people have decided to take the course even if they have not decided whether to go abroad or not. They just said that they wanted to improve their English. (16 April 005)

After her return from the test prep school, Yu tried to memorize three new lists of GRE words each day in order to finish all the lists. As there were a total of 51 lists, on a particular day she might have to review and memorize 24 lists of words, each list having around 100 words:

> I spent about ten days trying to memorize all the GRE words. [...] I used the Red book and memorized most of them. [...] Ten days, I just memorized these words. And I did nothing else. [...] Our teacher told us that we did not need to remember the words' pronunciation. Because we only used them in the exam and we did not have to read them. I just read all the sample sentences for three new wordlists for the day. For other lists that I should review for the day, I just read Chinese and English. I did not have time to read

all the sample sentences if I had to memorize 24 lists on one day. (17 September 2005)

Although Yu believed that such memorization efforts helped her to understand lectures better, the whole experience was utterly confusing and disorienting for her. She gave up her memorization effort even before she completed all the lists because she found the whole experience unbearable and her memorization effort useless. Like her early memorization efforts, she again failed to remember the words that were not frequently used in her studies and daily life. As she became increasingly busy with her architectural work, she no longer learnt English in this way. Asked whether she would do anything different from memorizing English words in the future, she answered:

> I would do something else. I do not want to torture myself again. I had tried to memorize GRE words. That was enough. I was really frightened. It had such negative effects on me. I may choose to read books or watch movies. (30 May 2006)

Yu's experience of memorizing GRE words again shows how her strategy use was mediated by contextual conditions. Driven by great uncertainties associated with her investment in academic studies and language learning, she put considerable effort into memorizing GRE words, which led her to some progress in learning English but more feelings of frustration. Memorizing GRE words was a desperate struggle for her to gain momentum in learning English since academic studies took up most of her time at the university. It was also the pinnacle of the conflict between her agency and contextual conditions in her language learning experiences in Hong Kong. She suffered from conflicting desires to have more English and better academic results, while she had to endure contextual constraints on her language learning efforts, such as the dominance of Cantonese in her design studio and group work activities. These constraints meant that she needed to put extra time and effort into creating and sustaining a social learning space to support her language learning efforts. Yet she did not have the required time and energy. Without a supportive social learning network, she was likely to be less effective in dealing with these constraints and conflicts to pursue English competence.

Mengshi

Mengshi was born into an educated professional family with his father having received higher education. His father personally taught him his first English words before sending him to a private tutor for better English instruction. Upon his graduation from secondary school, his parents decided to send him to Hong Kong for tertiary education. Based on his own account, he was one of those who were hard-working and motivated enough to achieve academic success through taking exams. He memorized test-preparation materials like many other Chinese students when he was in high school. During his preparatory year in a mainland Chinese university, he memorized words and prepared for the CET-4 test (College English Test, Band 4) to improve his English even though he did not have to take it as a Hong Kong-bound student. He appeared to be less critical about the learning context on the Chinese mainland than other participants in the study and, at the same time, he was vaguely uneasy about his ways of learning English. On the Chinese mainland, he spent some three to four hours a day learning English during the preparatory year, even though he felt he had made little progress in English.

Mengshi's account of learning English in Hong Kong is a tale of persistent effort and many failures. Like Liu and Yu, Mengshi wished to find employment upon graduation in Hong Kong and had to deal with the task of learning Cantonese in order to collaborate with local students in academic activities and daily life. Yet, to succeed in an English-medium university in Hong Kong, he knew that he had to have a good command of English. To achieve these aims, Mengshi consistently spent time learning English and Cantonese, at least in the first semester. While the university provided some opportunities for him to practise English and the hall was a good place for him to interact with local students in Cantonese, he felt that his progress in both languages was unsatisfactory. Nevertheless, he became increasingly active in seizing learning opportunities and was stoical in dealing with his failures. The following sections focus on his efforts to learn Cantonese by joining a softball team in the hall despite the enormous difficulty in identifying himself as one of the hall team (local students' group). In addition, we shall see the continuous efforts he made to create more opportunities to speak English and the various barriers that discouraged him. Finally, his ongoing English learning efforts will be analysed, including his vocabulary memorization in preparation for IELTS, which he felt did not help improve his English.

Socializing with local students

Mengshi's socialization experiences speak of the contextual constraints on his efforts in acquiring Cantonese and English. He lived in one of the most traditional residential halls for male students in the university. His residential membership came with a compulsory meal plan requiring him to have dinner together with other residents in the hall. The hall was renowned for its commitment to sports and student activities. Apart from his life at the hall, he had to participate in numerous student projects with other students, required by the academic programme he was undertaking. Like many other mainland Chinese students, Mengshi had been motivated to come to study in Hong Kong as a place with better career opportunities for economics and finance graduates. Therefore, he realized that he needed to learn Cantonese although his interest in Cantonese helped his motivation:

> I want to learn Cantonese. I think that it is necessary to learn Cantonese. [...] We mainland students will have to interact with local students. [...] In tutorials, they may discuss in Cantonese. Not (in) all of them but the ones I went to, they did. (2 October 2004)

> Actually, in my unconsciousness, I like to learn Cantonese. And I want to understand what people think in Cantonese. (5 February 2005)

The student hall was a good place for him to learn Cantonese as most of the social exchanges that took place there were in that language. To improve his Cantonese, Mengshi realized that he needed to integrate more into the hall community. For this purpose, he decided to join a sports team in the hall to 'know local students' (15 October 2004):

> Last week, I played softball with my hall mates. [...] You see, I want to try a new game [...] and also it helps me to have opportunities to communicate with local students. (2 October 2004)

The softball team membership gave him more opportunities to socialize with local students but also highlighted the cultural differences he had with some of them. One particular incident worth mentioning was circulated in the mainland Chinese students' online forum. Briefly put, Mengshi's hall softball team lost a game when playing against another hall. His team members became quite emotional at the end of the game. To make matters worse, the winning team started a series of war cries celebrating their achievement and deriding Mengshi's hall team's downfall. As a result, many local team members were reduced to tears of anger. Like most online commentators in the mainland Chinese students' forum, Mengshi could not understand why these local team members cried in front of others over a match:

> The warden said that it (the opponent team's cheering) was normal. Those things happen all the time. But the Hall softball team members (local students) cried. I did not cry myself. I don't know why. I do not pay too much attention to the game. I just took it as fun. Nothing

serious. Sometimes I cannot understand it. Why did they cry? [...]
They paid too much attention to it. [...] for me, I just wanted to try a
new game and then know some people. (19 November 2004)

The fact that the local students cried over their team losing a game reflects
how much they valued the importance of the community's honour, something that perhaps was not fully appreciated by Mengshi who regarded
himself as a supportive outsider. This widely noted incident among mainland Chinese undergraduates at the time was one of many reminding him
that there were considerable differences between his local counterparts
and himself, especially in terms of what they valued in life (Ho *et al.*, 2003;
Schack & Schack, 2005). In contrast to most of the local students in the hall
who liked to enjoy their youth and hall life to the utmost, Mengshi had a
totally different priority in his life and study:

After two months here, (I realized), if I do not work hard, it does not
make a difference for me whether I study in Hong Kong or not. [...] I
want to work here. A lot of mainland Chinese students want to work
here. Me, too. Or I want to go further abroad. [...] In order to achieve
them, I need to improve my languages, both Cantonese and English, I
need to do well in my academic subjects. (25 October 2004)

Although Mengshi always regarded his hall mates and the warden as nice
people, he repeatedly complained that the hall was 'too noisy' (23
December 2004; 29 January, 5 February 2005; 17 March, 29 April 2006)
because they liked to party till late. This cultural clash might have prevented him from becoming fully involved in the residential community:

I do not think that I am a XXX hall member. I am a friend to XXXians
(members of the XXX Hall) and my local friends. But I am reluctant to
be one of the XXXians because they are too noisy. (30 May 2006)

By the end of the longitudinal research, Mengshi had not acquired a com-
fortable level of Cantonese and did not appear to be confident in dealing
with local students and people in the language. He had tried but did not
go too far in Cantonese possibly because he was unable to see things as
local students did or, as a non-local student, he could not have the same
life priorities as his local counterparts. Without such shared understanding, it was hardly surprising to learn that he could not integrate well into
the community of local students and acquire a better command of
Cantonese. Unlike Liu, he failed to use local students as potential partners
in pursuing both Cantonese and English competence.

Challenges in utilizing social learning resources

As he was trying to improve his Cantonese, he committed himself to improving his spoken English competence by seizing every possible learning opportunity available in the residential hall and on the campus. He found that many local students in the hall could speak quite fluent English and so he attempted to have conversations in English with them after arrival in Hong Kong. However, it quickly became apparent that local students were more interested in using Putonghua in conversation with him:

> I don't have opportunities to speak English. [...] I tried to talk to local students in English in the hall but they tried to talk to me in Putonghua. [...] In my corridor, there are five people. Two are from the Chinese mainland. Three are trying to learn Putonghua. So Putonghua is the corridor language. (25 October 2004)

While the opportunities to use English with local students were limited, he had one or two exchange students on the same floor with whom he could practise his English. In the first semester, there was an ethnic Chinese student from Norway who could speak fluent Cantonese. However, Mengshi's efforts at using English with him were not well received by his mainland counterparts in the same residential hall, indicating the pressure he had to withstand when speaking English to other ethnic Chinese students:

> Sometimes I speak English to my hall mate. He is from Norway. Although we do not chat with each other very much, some mainland students look at us with strange expressions on their faces. (23 December 2004)

Such experience did not discourage him from using English with exchange students. The inquiry revealed that he frequently attempted to practise English with English-speaking non-local students, although conversations he managed to have with them were short and often limited to simple social exchanges in the beginning. The scope of his conversations expanded as he kept working on his English and engaged in reading newspapers. In the fourth semester, Mengshi met two exchange students, one from Norway and the other from Germany. He was able to have discussions about many topics with them although he was often at a loss when the two talked about something he had little knowledge about, such as football, popular music, politics and history. As a business study student, he probably lacked the linguistic resources and relevant knowledge to make contributions in such debates. Consequently, he did not find such learning

experiences satisfactory. Nevertheless, these were the best learning opportunities that he had ever had to improve his oral competence:

> [...] so we at least can have some daily conversation. [...] all sorts of
> things. Politics, which is news. College, professors. One of the stu-
> dents is from Germany. He is a kind of politics person. He is a law
> student. He always talks about politics. Other students talk about the
> Second World War and talk about some nationalists. [...] It is kind of
> very interesting. It is kind of strange. (1 April 2006)

In addition, Mengshi saw that the English medium instruction and constructive learning provided potential learning opportunities for him to
improve his oral competence. Group work, if done in English, provided
learning opportunities for him to improve his oral competence. However,
it was difficult for him to insist on using English in group discussions
when the group included local students who preferred Cantonese. He felt
that the 'wall' (differences) between local students and him made it difficult for him to choose English to communicate, as he would have liked:

> They (local students) preferred Cantonese but sometimes we use
> English. [...] I think that I would like to use Cantonese because maybe
> some local students felt uncomfortable about using English. I cannot
> determine which language is to be used. We can start with English
> discussion but during the discussion, somebody changes it to
> Cantonese. What can we do? [...] If I had a choice, I would probably
> choose English because my Cantonese is even worse. Of course, if we
> insist on using English, they will use English. But when they commu-
> nicate with each other, they will use Cantonese. It seems there is a
> wall between them and us. (11 March 2006)

Apart from his unsuccessful efforts to learn English through socializing
with other students, Mengshi practised using English with Liu for quite a
long time during the current study so that he could have some regular
English language-speaking opportunities. Another strategic decision he
made to improve his English was to join the longitudinal follow-up study
in order to have some regular opportunities to use English, albeit with a
non-native speaker. These strategic decisions indicate that he was highly
motivated to improve his oral English because many other mainland
Chinese students found it difficult and unusual to speak to another fellow
mainland Chinese in English. In this case, the English medium of the university might have helped him to justify his actions before others, especially mainland Chinese students:

> It is just quite natural for people to speak English, for example, when a
> professor speaks English, you want to raise a question, you will use

English. [...] I think that it is quite normal for mainlanders to speak English with mainlanders. Last week, I went to see my probability tutor who is a mainlander. I asked him questions in English. (12 March 2005)

Mengshi's strategic moves in utilizing possible social learning resources revealed his agency in his pursuit of English competence, in particular oral competence. In this regard, he had displayed persistence in his ongoing efforts to create a supportive niche for his language learning efforts, including his use of social strategies. However, his efforts in seeking and creating language learning and use opportunities were constrained by the linguistic reality in Hong Kong and the dominance of Cantonese as the socialization medium in contrast to English as the instruction medium (Davison & Lai, 2007; Keung, 2006). In addition, his lack of knowledge in relation to issues being discussed might have prevented him from fully participating in the interaction with exchange students and hence benefiting from such language use opportunities. As a result, in his eyes, his learning efforts failed to produce the success he desired.

Struggle to learn more English

Apart from improving his oral competence, Mengshi consistently worked to raise his general English level. He understood that he needed to 'do a lot of things' in order to learn English (25 October 2004). The problem was that he often appeared to do many things without much conviction about whether they actually worked or not. At the beginning, like many other mainland Chinese students in Hong Kong, he endeavoured to improve his listening comprehension and increase his vocabulary knowledge. To this end, he read newspapers to learn new words in context and listened to English tapes he had brought from the Chinese mainland. However, he did not think that these strategies worked well 'because I tried to memorize words from reading ... (which) did not work very well' (2 October 2004, English original). Nevertheless, he still continued using these strategies, hoping that he could improve his English in this way:

> Before I go to bed, I can have some thirty minutes or three quarters on learning English. I normally listen to tapes. And at the weekend, I learn some vocabulary and read some newspaper. I don't memorize vocabulary. I just go through the newspaper and learn some new words. I take them down, which I did not do on the Chinese mainland. I found it very important to learn English but also I found it useless to learn it. I don't know why. Sometimes, I always forgot the new words I learnt (Gao: You probably never use the words you learnt.) But the problem is where can I find places to use them? (6 November 2006)

As he progressed in his academic studies, he gradually overcame the listening barrier and subsequently devoted less time to improving his listening comprehension. At the same time, his extensive reading took on new meaning. He was initially motivated to read English to expand his vocabulary but later on he engaged in reading to increase his knowledge about the world and considered it an important opportunity to use the knowledge acquired from his academic discipline to interpret events in the world:

> Sometimes I just keep on finding interesting news. Maybe I did not learn new vocabulary. Interesting news about politics and economy. [...] Reading the newspaper also helps me to understand economics. But sometimes some critical words cause problems. So I try to learn these words. (5 March 2005)

In addition, high-stakes examinations were an important motivating factor compelling him to put time and effort into learning English. In this respect, the popular ways of learning English among mainland Chinese students left a clear imprint on Mengshi's language learning efforts. In 2005, he spent a substantial amount of time memorizing words for IELTS, a test that he believed that he must take if he wanted to go for exchange studies a year later. That summer, he went to take a test preparation course in Shanghai for IELTS when Yu was taking a GRE preparation course in Beijing. Like other participants, he also had a book containing many wordlists for IELTS to memorize, although he found it very difficult to memorize them:

> It is very hard to learn those words in the IELTS wordlist. There are seven thousand of them. [...] I spend an hour or half in the morning and also in the evening every day on memorizing words. (24 September 2005)

Moreover, he also had to deal with the conflict between language learning efforts and academic studies. Starting from his second academic year in Hong Kong, he found that it was increasingly difficult for him to control his time. As a result, although he completed one round of memorization of the wordlists in 14 days, he could not continue his memorization efforts because 'I am always short of time this semester' (22 October 2005, English original). He was then disappointed to discover that his memorization efforts did not pay off at all:

> I have forgotten all the vocabulary I had memorized this semester. That is terrible. [...] After spending a year, I do not think that I have made any progress (in English)! (16 November 2005)

However, in spite of the priority that Mengshi gave to academic studies whenever they clashed with learning English, he began to view progress in learning English as fundamental to his pursuit of an ideal self. Though he might have been strongly committed to the learning of English, for quite a long time he saw English as an academic subject that he should succeed in and lacked the strong will that Liu and Zhixuan demonstrated in their accounts of learning English. However, one might argue that Mengshi was definitely not the only mainland student who had such an attitude to the learning of English. Like many other mainland Chinese students, he often found it difficult to struggle with the demands for English proficiency and academic performance in relation to his future employment. Both demanded a substantial amount of time and were needed to make him more employable:

Gao: What is your ideal self?
Mengshi: First, I can speak English fluently and confidently. Maybe I can have excellent academic results. Third, I can find a good job here.
Gao: So English is more important than your academic study and job?
Mengshi: Yes, it is necessary for everything. Academic results will give you an opportunity to promote yourself but how to promote yourself will depend on your English level. (5 December 2005)

Realizing that his progress in English was far from satisfactory, Mengshi felt that he was denied one of the most integral parts of the ideal self that he wished to achieve, casting a dark shadow on his life and study in Hong Kong. Reflecting on his language learning experiences, I must point out that he did make some progress in learning English, for instance, his listening comprehension. However, he seemed to concentrate much of his learning efforts on memorizing words or reading English materials for new vocabulary, suggestive of his belief in learning a language as acquiring blocks of vocabulary and grammatical points (Benson & Lor, 1999). This might be interpreted as an indication of some deficiency in his conception of language learning, but his focus on memorization might have been associated with his failure (dissatisfaction) in utilizing social learning resources at the university. Throughout the inquiry, he knew that it was important to learn the language through socialization, but he failed to build supportive social networks, which would have enabled him to use social strategies to experience growth in his English competence. Furthermore, academic studies also made it impossible for him to spend the regular amount of time and effort on socialization (as in the case of Yu).

Context and Agency in the Participants' Narratives

This chapter has presented four case study participants' experiential narratives of strategy use in acquiring English, revealing the underlying interaction of agency and context. Together with the findings in Chapters 4 and 5, they help create a meta-story of the participants' strategy use in an English-medium university in Hong Kong that can be interpreted at four different levels, namely the contextual, institutional, interaction and individual levels (see Figure 2.5).

At the contextual level, these accounts reveal that the participants dealt with complex linguistic issues and cultural differences in their language learning and educational pursuits. The fluid linguistic complexity in Hong Kong required them to be ideally competent in both English and Cantonese as English plays an important sociopolitical function and Cantonese is the dominant medium for socialization. At the institutional level, the dominance of Cantonese on the campus and the collaborative learning approach tended to oblige many mainland undergraduates to acquire Cantonese in order to integrate into the student community. At the same time, the English medium instruction of the university also compelled them to improve their English. However, mediated by the wider sociocultural and political processes at the contextual level, the tasks of learning the two languages were often in conflict with each other. The learning of languages also competed with academic studies, the most important task in their perception, for time and effort from the participants. Consequently, at the level of interaction, the participants attempted to utilize resources in the new learning setting and broaden their engagement in acquiring English competence. The sociocultural barriers that they had with local students, exacerbated by the fact that most of them did not speak Cantonese, made them become more likely to be isolated. For this reason, three of the case study participants tried to learn Cantonese initially and integrate themselves into the student community. However, they found that opportunities to learn and use English decreased as their Cantonese improved while their integration efforts were often frustrated by the existing cultural differences between them and their local counterparts (Ho *et al.*, 2003; Schack & Schack, 2005), indicating the mediation of existing contextual conditions. In their pursuit of educational objectives, they also found that academic studies put further constraints on the amount of time and effort that they could put in learning languages.

At the individual level, these contextual and institutional realities played an important role in mediating each case study participant's experiences of language learning and strategy use in Hong Kong. The four case study participants differ from each other in terms of their language learning experiences and strategy use, which suggests the role of agency in each participant's learning. Upon further reflection, the differences among these participants can be attributed to different values, beliefs, knowledge and capacity that they had in learning English. For instance, Liu and Zhixuan, in comparison with Yu and Mengshi, clearly articulated a connection between English competence and their identity to sustain their learning efforts throughout the inquiry while Yu and Mengshi were less certain about the utility of their learning efforts although they persisted in undertaking them. Although Liu and Zhixuan did regard the learning of English as an important means to gain access to other resources and cultural capital (Norton Peirce, 1995), the rewards that they expected to have also included self-enrichment. In spite of moments of uncertainty and frustration, both learners were largely able to focus on their self-growth and experience a learning process with their 'will' to learn and use English being continuously sustained rather than undermined. Hence, to cope with contextual constraints, Liu and Zhixuan might have different responses from Yu and Mengshi. For instance, even though the enduring 'us–them' differences she had with local students might have prevented her from participating fully in the student community, Liu persisted in taking these strategic efforts in spite of her psychological distancing from the community resulting from early failures.

In addition, they also differed in their skills and capacity to cope with contextual conditions. Although they may all have similar understanding of the context for the learning of the language, Liu and Zhixuan seem to have been more skilful in identifying suitable peers, recruiting them into a supportive learning network and maintaining such social learning space for their language learning efforts. While Liu and Zhixuan were good at trading their expertise for language practice opportunities, that is, Putonghua for Liu and chemistry knowledge for Zhixuan, Yu and Mengshi rarely reported similar learning experiences. Yu might have found it nearly impossible to invest time and efforts in learning English and having a supportive social space because of the particularly heavy coursework load and learning organization. Mengshi might have also lacked appropriate sociocultural knowledge to allow his continuous participation in social learning networks as he often found it difficult to engage in conversations with exchange students on particular topics. Yu and Mengshi, like many other participants in the study, did use high-stakes examinations to create a learning condition in which they could mobilize their efforts to learn more English. What distinguished them from Liu and Zhixuan in terms of the quality of their language learning experiences could be their limited capacities in constructing and transforming contextual learning conditions to achieve their language learning objectives.

Conclusion

Together with the preceding chapter, these narratives reveal that the participants benefited from rich learning resources and learning opportunities in the new learning context but that they also had difficulties in negotiating and maintaining their access to these learning opportunities. The data indicate that the participants' readiness and willingness to endure or circumvent the contextual conditions were critical in their pursuit of linguistic competence and mediated their satisfaction with their learning investment. The findings support the argument that those who are satisfied with their language learning progress are likely to be those who are able to successfully create and maintain a supportive social learning space for their language learning efforts.

Chapter 7
Agency and Context in Strategic Learning

In the previous chapters, I have reported on an inquiry conducted in three phases on a group of mainland Chinese undergraduates' language learning experiences on the Chinese mainland and in Hong Kong. Drawing on sociocultural language learning research, the inquiry explored the dynamic relationship between the participants' strategy use and changing learning contexts. This chapter summarizes the main contributions that the inquiry may have with regard to the field of LLS research and discusses their implications for pedagogy and research. As strategy research is often related to researchers' interest in devising programmes to support and develop language learners, this chapter places particular emphasis on the contention that the findings from this inquiry broaden the current understanding of language learners' strategic learning and lend support to an expanded vision of learner development programmes.

Overall Findings

In Chapter 4, I described 22 participants' language learning experiences on the Chinese mainland and how their strategic learning efforts had been mediated by contextual conditions. Then I identified patterns of, as well as shifts in, their strategy use during the pre-Hong Kong year. The next step was a demonstration of how the participants were exposed to the mediation of various social agents, including parents, teachers and peers in the previous learning process. I also examined the dominant societal and traditional discourses in their motivational discourses about learning English and the mediation of cultural artefacts such as high-stakes examinations on their learning experiences.

In Chapter 5, in the light of the baseline findings from the study in Phase 1, the inquiry in Phase 3 revealed both shifts and continuity in the participants' strategy use. Underlying these shifts there were changes in the participants' discourses about language learning, in that they appeared to have diverse learning motives, including cultural motives, and yet, at the same time, they had further internalized the traditional discourses in Chinese culture and were exposed to the mediation of the societal discourses in Hong Kong, both attaching instrumental value to language learning. While rich material resources in the new learning context had certainly facilitated these changes in the participants' learning efforts and learning discourses, their socialization experiences with local peers were indicative of contextual realities, including linguistic complexity and sociocultural gaps, which they had to cope with in the language learning process. Chapters 4 and 5 present an overall snapshot of the participants' shifting strategy use as a group and also describe the interaction of agency and context underlying these changes.

Chapter 6 focused on four longitudinal case study participants' experiential accounts of learning in Hong Kong, highlighting the strategic responses that these participants had to the particular benefits and constraints that they experienced when learning English in Hong Kong. These responses were often strategic decisions to utilize opportunities and/or bypass contextual constraints in the new learning context. These strategic decisions played an important role in the participants' use of particular strategies at different stages of their learning career in Hong Kong, highlighting the role of agency in learners' strategic learning efforts. From an approach different from that in Chapters 4 and 5, this chapter provides an in-depth analysis of how the study participants' agency interacted with contextual conditions in their pursuit of linguistic competence.

Agency, Context and Strategic Learning

Use of a sociocultural perspective enabled the inquiry to move beyond a limited focus on individual language learners and their cognitive learning process, bringing in new conceptions of learner, learning, context and LLS, and situating their strategy use in particular learning contexts. Given this, the answers to the research questions that frame the research are rather complex. The inquiry not only identified some shifts in the participants' strategy use, but also revealed certain resilience in the patterns of strategy use after arrival in Hong Kong. These findings suggest that there is an ongoing interaction between context and agency underlying the participants' strategy use. This is to say that, if 'choice' is a defining character of learners' strategic learning behaviour (Cohen, 1998: 4), then learners' strategy use is often a mediated choice, but nevertheless it remains the learners' choice. The following sections highlight the relevant findings from the inquiry and discuss their potential contributions to LLS research.

Strategy use as a mediated choice: The role of learning contexts

Previous strategy research recognizes that learning context mediates language learners' strategy use (e.g. Nyikos & Oxford, 1993; Oxford & Nyikos, 1989), but previous LLS research lacks an articulation and critical conceptualization of context. In contrast, sociocultural LLS research calls for a shift in theorizing context (Norton & Toohey, 2001) and sees context as being fundamental to learners' learning (Zuengler & Miller, 2006). This study examined how learning contexts, seen as a combination of culture, discourses, social agents and material resources or artefacts (Donato & McCormick, 1994; Palfreyman, 2006), mediated the participants' language learning efforts. Drawing on the sociocultural interpretative framework (Figure 2.5), the inquiry investigated how different layers of contextual reality, including macro-social context and micro-institutional setting, as well as interaction taking place between participants and contextual elements, affected their learner actions (i.e. their strategy use).

The findings in the inquiry support the view that learning contexts mediated the participants' strategy use in learning English and the learning discourses underlying their strategy use. For instance, the participants' parents worked closely with teachers to imbue them with the societal and traditional learning discourses, including 'English is a tool', which became a motivational force driving them to memorize words, grammar points and texts for high-stakes examinations on the Chinese mainland. The abundance of learning resources in Hong Kong encouraged them to use strategies to increase their exposure to English. As another example, high-stakes examinations, as cultural artefacts, mediated the participants to use exam-oriented learning strategies on the Chinese mainland and in Hong Kong. These examples indicate that contextual realities, such as increasingly competitive educational processes and cultural emphasis on the pragmatic values of education, influenced the participants to adopt particular strategies. Thus, these findings underscore the important role that learning contexts have in mediating learners' strategy choices (Donato & McCormick, 1994; Norton & Toohey, 2001) and support sociocultural LLS researchers' criticisms of earlier LLS research presenting learners' strategy use as 'largely pertaining to individual will and knowledge' (Parks &

Raymond, 2004: 375). In other words, learners' strategy use is often a con-strained choice or choice made possible by learning contexts.

Learners' strategy use is still a choice: The role of agency

Although the findings indicate that the participants' strategy use was mediated by contextual realities, they do not negate the importance of learner agency in their strategy use in acquiring English, but rather provide a nuanced understanding of learner agency captured in their accounts. Learners' strategy use is related to their exercise of power, the will and capacity to act otherwise, and their strategy use reveals their agency in the learning process. The inquiry investigated what constituted their power, and the will and capacity to act otherwise in the learning process. It also revealed that the participants reflected and constructed the meanings of contextual realities in relation to them.

In addition, the findings indicate that the participants were able to criti-cally reflect on the impact of exam-oriented strategy use and popular exam-related learning discourses on their language learning. Their adop-tion of exam-oriented learning strategies was deliberate and intentional, reflected in the fact that many of them chose exam-oriented learning strat-egies in later learning stages, namely during the preparatory year and during their stay in Hong Kong, when there were no compulsory exami-nations. Differences among the participants' strategy use and language learning experiences in Hong Kong also speak for the role of agency in the learning process. The study also revealed that some participants were par-ticularly creative in their attempts to overcome or bypass contextual con-straints on their language learning. For instance, Liu was able to create and sustain a social network supporting her language learning efforts through manipulating the relationships between Cantonese, English and Putonghua. In contrast, Mengshi found it extremely difficult to have sus-tainable access to such supportive social learning resources. These differ-ences in the participants' will and capacity to act otherwise (Giddens, 1976, 1984) led to diverse perceptions of learning contexts and different levels of satisfaction over their learning progress among the participants.

Conceptualizing agency in relation to the participants' use of power, this study addresses the reservation that Wenden (1998: 530) had about sociocultural language learning research in regard to the 'underdevel-oped' role of learner agency in the learning process. The findings develop the concept 'learner agency' in sociocultural LLS research and support an argument that it should be broadened to include a number of elements other than learners' metacognitive knowledge (Wenden, 1998, 2002) or self-regulatory competence (Tseng *et al.*, 2006). Language learners are more likely to realize the potential of their LLS knowledge in the learning process if they have an appropriate level of sociocultural capacity, including a critical understanding of particular social learning contexts and identification of contextual elements for reconfiguration. Their critical appreciation of learning contexts helps them to acquire knowledge of valuable social and cultural practices that could be used by the participants to sustain their access to social learning opportunities. For instance, Zhixuan's familiarity with American culture, although limited, proved to be instrumental in his socialization with American exchange students in Hong Kong and the United States. In contrast, Mengshi's lack of knowledge of history or pop music became barriers in his socialization with exchange students. Moreover, acting upon such understanding of the context and knowledge of valuable practices, the participants' micro-political moves contribute to the participants' learning satisfaction in the findings. It was found in the inquiry that the participants who were satisfied with their experiences of learning English often turned out to be those who were good at relating to local or other non-local students and recruiting them as valuable social support for their language learning efforts (e.g. Liu and Zhixuan). As a result, in comparison with other participants, these participants were more often able to transform contextual conditions and create favourable social networks to support their language learning efforts. Finally, participants like Liu and Zhixuan displayed an unwavering belief in the importance of English in their future life and identity construction and attached a mixture of instrumental and cultural values to the learning of it, which resulted from a long socialization process mediated by various social agents and artefacts in both contexts. Therefore, this study has helped identify a variety of capacities and a motive/belief system as the participants' agency underlying their active strategy use and satisfactory learning.

A sociocultural proposal for learner development

Without negating the importance of agency, the sociocultural research perspective in this inquiry allows a critical examination of the contextual mediation on their strategy use, a lack in most LLS research deplored by Parks and Raymond (2004) (also see Norton & Toohey, 2001). In fact, as the study probed into different layers of contextual realities in relation to the participants' strategy use, it helped reveal the extraordinary will and capacity that language learners may need to mobilize as well as utilize to achieve learning success. Apart from strategic learning capacity, the language learner needs to be empowered with both sociocultural and micro-political capacity as well as strong motives and beliefs about learning English. In particular, the participants' high motivation could be explained by their ongoing exposure to the societal and traditional discourses about learning, their awareness of social competition and an enduring belief in the importance of learning as a means to achieve social mobility. In other words, they saw learning efforts as a form of investment (Bai, 2006; Norton Peirce, 1995). For this reason, investment of learning efforts requires rational calculations on the part of the participants because investment means risk and uncertainty. This possibly explains why the participants found it problematic to deal with language learning and academic studies in Hong Kong. Their accounts of language learning efforts are also suggestive of their attempts to seek assurance for something that is uncertain.

The contributions to LLS research made by the findings from the study can be further illustrated by a sociocultural proposal for LLS research and development, which reveals an interactive process between learner agency and contextual conditions, as represented by Figure 7.1. The illustration locates learner agency within immediate settings and broad sociocultural contexts with learners' strategy use connecting 'agency' and 'setting'. Constituting elements in 'setting' interact with different components of learner agency (power) while 'context' seems to have indirect interaction with learner agency through 'setting'. Different components of learners' power, their will and capacity, also interact with each other. Thus, a dynamic picture of learners' strategy use as a mediated choice emerges.

Although the illustration points to contextual conditions as the root problem for language learners' learning, it does not negate the importance of seeking solutions at the level of learner agency. The findings indicate that variations in their socialization experiences in both contexts may lead to differences in their capacities as well as the underlying motive/belief system, which in turn lead to variations in their actual strategy use and satisfaction with their learning efforts. They also show that an enormous amount of effort is needed to empower language learners with the appropriate will and capacities to endure and deal with conditions in particular learning contexts. In other words, the findings remind researchers that the solution to the problems encountered by language learners similar to those of the study participants cannot be reached by focusing on language learners alone; it needs a concerted effort involving both language learners and various social agents who both directly and indirectly mediate language learners' learning efforts. Therefore, language teachers and researchers need to become committed to an expanded notion of learner

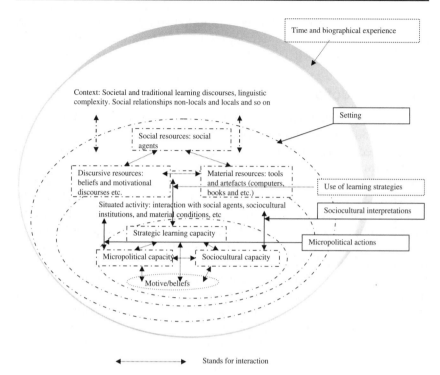

Figure 7.1 A sociocultural perspective on language learners' strategic learning

development effort that enhances a variety of capacities as well as a motive/belief system among learners.

In short, this interpretive inquiry into mainland Chinese undergraduates' accounts of strategic language learning efforts on the Chinese mainland and in Hong Kong contributes to the increasing research literature on learners learning languages in specific social, historical and cultural contexts (Block, 2003; Morgan, 2007; Zuengler & Miller, 2006). In particular, it adds to a limited number of empirical studies dealing with 'emergence of strategy use as a process directly connected to the practices of cultural groups' (Donato & McCormick, 1994: 453, also see Parks & Raymond, 2004). Moreover, the inquiry has addressed some of the criticisms that have been leveled against sociocultural LLS research. It has examined the ongoing interaction between context and agency underlying the participant's strategy use and developed the concept of agency (power) for future sociocultural LLS inquiries. Concerning the practical question of how language learners might be supported, the findings argue for an expanded notion of learner development fostering a variety of capacities as well as a motive/belief system.

Recommendations

This study started with a practical concern: thousands of Chinese students abroad are in need of support schemes that help them to survive and succeed in new learning contexts. Exploring the participants' language learning experiences and strategy use, the study has now concluded that learner development effort, if limited to learners' strategic learning capacity, be it metacognitive knowledge (e.g. Wenden, 1998, 2002) or self-regulatory capacity (Dörnyei, 2005; Tseng *et al.*, 2006), seems to be insufficient for migrating students like the participants in the inquiry to endure the challenges in new contexts for successful learning. New learner development effort needs to be based on the understanding of strategy use resulting from the interaction between learner agency and context. This demands a shift of focus from individual language learners' capacity for strategic learning to their capacities in opening up and sustaining a social learning space for exercising their strategic learning capacity or utilizing their strategic learning knowledge. In specific terms, the shifts must be to

(1) Learners' sociocultural capacity, which enables them to appreciate the making and contemporary practices of a particular learning context. It helps them to identify appropriate contextual elements for reconfiguration so that their language learning efforts can be supported by more facilitative contextual conditions. Learners' sociocultural capacity also includes knowledge of valued social and cultural practices required by them to sustain their social exchanges with other social agents. In many senses, learners need to become good ethnographic researchers (or social researchers in Norton Peirce, 1995) in the first place so that they can adopt appropriate strategic responses in a particular learning context.

(2) Micro-political capacity, which allows them to utilize supportive elements and agents for their own language learning as well as to establish and maintain facilitative learning networks or communities in the context. Micro-political moves are most likely to be successful if they are based on a sound evaluation of the context. In this sense, learners are more likely to be successful if they can be both good diplomats and excellent ethnographic researchers.

(3) Language learners' motive/belief system, which constitutes one of the most critical parts of learner agency. It relates to the meanings and

values that language learners attach to their strategy use, educational investment and more broadly to other life pursuits. In most cases, language learners acquire such a motive/belief system after extended exposure to the societal and traditional discourses about learning and education through various social agents' mediation practices (Oxford, 1996). They contain the principles that learners use to construct meanings, and, in turn, mediate their will underlying different aspects of their agency, as well as their strategy use. Although no dramatic changes in learners' motive/belief system should be expected, the model does indicate interaction among different aspects of learners' agency. Hence, a continuous examination and re-examination may help learners to re-adjust their motive/belief systems (Yang, 1999) and enhance their endurance in learning contexts where they are often likely to have unsatisfactory and discouraging learning experiences, seriously undermining their strategy use.

Such learner development effort does not predict success in its potential impact on the language learner since it operates within particular contextual conditions. In addition, probably many meaningful interventions to develop language learners would take a long time to see their effects. However, language teachers may be comforted by the realization that they are not alone in the effort to help language learners to learn better. For instance, the study identified the importance of developing teacher–parent partnerships in implementing learner development programmes for young learners. If parents can be enabled to guide and supervise their child's language learning more effectively by such family–school/teacher–parent partnerships, language teachers may receive crucial assistance from parents who spend a much longer time with their children and have a strong emotional attachment to them. If we could pass on some of the wealth of knowledge about learner development in accessible forms to parents and other social agents, we would contribute to the creation of a wider social environment facilitating learners' language learning and development.

Further Research

The current inquiry has investigated mainland Chinese students' strategic learning efforts on the Chinese mainland in Hong Kong; it is an exploratory study that has a number of methodological limitations, including the limited number and range of the study participants. However, in spite of these methodological limitations, this study has generated a research narrative highlighting learning strategy use resulting from the ongoing interaction between learner agency and context. The contextual constraints and difficulties that the study participants had to deal with in the learning process may be similar to the challenges faced by many other students from various cultural contexts, who pursue English-medium education away from their home countries. As 'the element of choice' gives a special character to learning strategy in comparison with other non-strategic learning behaviour (Cohen, 1998: 4), there is a need to know more about how learners make mediated choices in strategy use in particular contexts. Moreover, this study is also an attempt to examine how language learners' strategy use is engendered by the interaction between learner agency and learning contexts, leading to further refinement in a more holistic approach to empower language learners in similar contexts. To this end, there are many more issues that need to be addressed in future research.

Firstly, further research into learners' interaction with various social agents, including teachers, family and peers, is needed to improve our understanding of learner development in a broader context than the classroom setting. For instance, parental involvement in young learners' development is clearly becoming a research priority as an increasing number of learners start learning English at younger ages and the contexts for developing these young learners are ever more diverse. Language learners' out-of-class learning activities should also be systematically explored and documented with particular focus on their efforts to sustain their learning by creating learning communities and seeking assistance among peers. In addition, comparative studies are needed for language learners who pursue English-medium education in contexts where the dominant language is not English. Findings from such studies are also applicable to learners in English-medium institutions in English-speaking contexts as many such learners often live in social circles dominated by languages other than English. Moreover, of particular relevance to this study, future researchers may need to recognize the diversity of Chinese learners. While this particular study focuses on some 'elite' learners of similar ethnic backgrounds, future research needs to explore language learning experiences of Chinese learners of various ethnic and regional backgrounds, in particular those from less well-off families, to see how they overcome constraints on their language learning in the learning process. Finally, recognizing the importance of context, one of the most important research aims for strategy researchers is to explore how the notion of agency can be further developed to shed light on learners' strategic learning efforts to enhance their learning in response to particular contexts.

Conclusion

The book reported on an inquiry exploring mainland Chinese under-graduates' language learning experiences on the Chinese mainland and in Hong Kong, with a focus on their strategy use in acquiring English. Taking different conceptions of learner, learning, context and LLS from those in previous LLS research, the inquiry sees learners' strategy use as a con-strained choice resulting from an ongoing interaction process between agency and context. It has demonstrated how contextual realities and pro-cesses mediated the participants' strategy use and how the participants adopted strategic efforts in response to these realities and processes, revealing their agency underlying their strategy use. While learners' stra-tegic learning efforts like many other human actions are results 'partly of man's freewill and partly of the law of inevitability' (Tolstoy, 1991: 1293), there are still reasons to believe that their struggles can lead to success if they act on appropriate and critical knowledge of learning contexts and social agents involved in the process, including themselves, as advised by Sun Tsu, the greatest Chinese military strategist. Consequently, these find-ings call for an expanded notion of learner development, which shifts the focus on individual learners' strategic learning capacity to the capacities needed by learners to open up and maintain a sustainable learning space for the deployment of such strategic learning capacity. In most cases, lan-guage learners will experience setbacks and failures in their pursuit of linguistic competence and as a result, the findings in the study also draw our attention to appreciate the importance of motive/belief systems, which help learners to sustain their efforts. More research is needed to explore language learners' strategic learning efforts resulting from the interaction between agency and context so that our effort to empower language learners can be refined holistically and benefits a variety of language learners facing similar challenges to those of the participants in this book.

Appendix 1: Interview Guide for the Arriving Mainland Chinese Undergraduates

(1) Opening questions:
   (a) How do they feel about studying in Hong Kong?
   (b) How did they come here?
   (c) What do they think about differences in studying in Hong Kong and mainland China.
   (d) What kind of challenges do they think that they are facing?
   (e) How do they feel about their English?
(2) English learning questions asking the learners to describe their current strategy use in general.
   (a) What do you think that you are learning English for?
   (b) What is the most important thing in learning English?
   (c) What are your targets in learning English? Why?
   (d) What kind of progress do you think that you will make in learning English here?
   (e) Describe how you learn English.
   (f) What kind of problems do you normally have in learning English?
   (g) What do you do to improve your speaking, listening, writing, reading, etc., normally?
   (h) Are you happy with your English?
   (i) What kind of help do you need most?
(3) Experiential questions:
   (a) Could you share with me your past language learning experiences?
   (b) When did you start learning English?

(c) What did you think about learning English at that time?
(d) What was learning English like at that time?
(e) What did you normally do in English classes?
(f) Any memorable event?
(g) Any memorable people?
(h) What kind of problems did you normally have in learning English at that time?
(i) How did you solve them at that time?
(j) Were you happy with your English at that time?
(k) What did you think that you had learnt there?
(l) What kind of help did you think that you needed most there?
(m) Did you get enough help? From whom? How did they help you?
(n) Other relevant questions.
(4) Closing questions:
(a) What kind of support do you expect to have?
(b) Are you willing to participate in a follow-up study?

Appendix 2: The Exit Interview Guide for Mainland Chinese Undergraduates

(1) How well are you doing with learning English so far?

(2) Comparing you of today and you at the time when we first met, what changes have you made in the two years?

(3) Do the differences include your English or Cantonese? In what way has your current level of English (or Cantonese) been meaningful to who you are today?

(4) How is your Cantonese? How did you improve your Cantonese? Why did you feel that you have to work on Cantonese?

(5) How did you get on with your English learning here during these years?

(6) Have you improved your English while working on your academic subjects through English medium of instruction or spending specially allocated time on your English?

(7) Why are you particularly motivated to learn English at the University? Were you motivated in similar ways when you were on the Chinese mainland?

(8) Which particular aspects of English did you think you had problems with? Which particular aspects of English have you been mainly working on for improvement?

(9) Why do you think that you have not done much about particular areas of English although you feel you have problems with them?

(10) What have you been doing in order to improve your English?

(11) Which particular aspects of English do you think you still have problems with? What kind of activities or behaviors do you normally

associate with the idea of learning English? Are they the same as those you had on the Chinese mainland?

(12) How much time do you normally spend on learning English? Or how much time do you think you spend on learning English? Was it always the same during the two years?

(13) Are there any periods that you found yourself particularly involved in learning English? Why was it so?

(14) You did have some plans for learning English after your arrival in Hong Kong. How did you carry out those plans? Or do you often think of planning and monitoring your learning progress? Or do you think that your English learning is well organized by yourself? Did you have plans to supervise your own learning progress on the Chinese mainland?

(15) What do you think of Hong Kong's English learning environment? In comparison with mainland or overseas countries?

(16) Are there any friends, teachers or other people who have influenced your language learning a lot? If so, can you give me more details?

(17) Do you have any experiences of feeling that you have solved some big problems in learning English? How did you feel at that time? Why?

(18) How do you relate such experiences to your later English learning experiences at the University?

(19) Do you think that English will be important for you in the future? In what ways?

(20) Any memorable individuals or things related to your English learning in Hong Kong?

(21) Any overall comments on your being a student and learning English here?

References

Adamson, B. (1998) English in China: The junior secondary school curriculum 1949–94. Unpublished doctoral thesis, The University of Hong Kong.

Adamson, B. (2002) Barbarian as a foreign language: English in China's schools. *World Englishes* 21, 231–243.

Anderson, N. (2005) L2 strategy research. In E. Hinkel (ed.) *Handbook of Research in Second Language Teaching and Learning* (pp. 757–774). Mahwah, NJ: Lawrence Erlbaum.

Atkinson, D. (2002) Toward a sociocognitive approach to second language acquisition. *The Modern Language Journal* 86, 525–545.

Bai, L. (2005) *Shaping the Ideal Child: Children and their Primers in Late Imperial China.* Hong Kong: Chinese University Press.

Bai, L. (2006) Graduate unemployment: Dilemmas and challenges in China's move to mass higher education. *The China Quarterly* 185, 128–144.

Bedell, D.A. and Oxford, R.L. (1996) Cross-cultural comparisons of language learning strategies in the People's Republic of China and other countries. In R.L. Oxford (ed.) *Language Learning Strategies Around the World: Cross-Cultural Perspectives* (pp. 47–60) (Technical Report no. 13). Honolulu: University of Hawaii, Second Language Teaching & Curriculum Center.

Benson, P. (1997) Language rights and the medium of instruction policy in Hong Kong. *Hong Kong Journal of Applied Linguistics* 2 (2), 1–21.

Benson, P. (2001) *Teaching and Researching Autonomy in Language Learning.* Harlow: Longman.

Benson, P. and Gao, X. (2008) Individual variation and language learning strategies. In S. Hurd and T. Lewis (eds) *Language Learning Strategies in Independent Settings* (pp. 25–40). Bristol: Multilingual Matters.

Benson, P. and Lor, W. (1999) Conceptions of language and language learning. *System* 27, 459–472.

Block, E. (1986) The comprehension strategies of second language readers. *TESOL Quarterly* 20, 463–494.

Block, D. (2003) *The Social Turn in Second Language Acquisition.* Edinburgh: Edinburgh University.

Bolton, K. (2002) Chinese Englishes: From Canton jargon to global English. *World Englishes* 21, 181–192.

Bolton, K. and Lim, S. (2000) Futures for Hong Kong. *World Englishes* 19, 429–443.

Bourdieu, P. (1986) The forms of capital. In J. Richardson (ed.) *Handbook of Theory and Research for the Sociology of Education* (pp. 241–258), New York: Greenwood Press.

Boyle, J. (1997) Imperialism and the English language in Hong Kong. *Journal of Multilingual and Multicultural Development* 18, 169–181.

Carson, J.G. and Longhini, A. (2002) Focusing on learning styles and strategies: A diary study in an immersion setting. *Language Learning* 52, 401–438.

Carter, B. and New, C. (2004) *Make Realism Work: Realist Social Theory and Empirical Research*. New York: Routledge.

Case, E. (2004) *Making the Transition from an Intensive English Program to Mainstream University Courses: An Ethnographic Study*. Lewiston: Edwin Mellen Press.

Chamot, A.U. (2001) The role of learning strategies in second language acquisition. In M. Breen (ed.) *Learner Contributions to Language Learning* (pp. 25–43). Harlow: Pearson Education.

Chamot, A.U. (2004) Issues in language learning strategy research and teaching. *Electronic Journal of Foreign Language Teaching* 1, 14–26.

Chamot, A.U., Dale, M., O'Malley, J.M. and Spanos, G. (1992) Learning and problem solving strategies of ESL students. *Bilingual Research Journal* 16 (3&4), 1–34.

Cheng, X. (2000) Asian students' reticence revisited. *System* 28, 435–446.

Cho, J. and Trent, A. (2006) Validity in qualitative research revisited. *Qualitative Research* 6, 319–340.

Cohen, A. (1998) *Strategies in Learning and Using Second Language*. Harlow: Longman.

Cohen, A. and Macaro, E. (2007) *Language Learner Strategies*. Oxford: Oxford University Press.

Cohen, L., Manion, L. and Morrison, K. (2000) *Research Methods in Education*. London: Routledge Falmer.

Cohen, A., Oxford, R.L. and Chi, J. (2006) Language strategy use survey. On WWW at http://www.carla.umn.edu/about/profiles/CohenPapers/Lg_Strat_Srvy.html. Accessed 26.02.2007.

Corson, D. (1991) Bhaskar's critical realism and educational knowledge. *British Journal of Sociology of Education* 12, 223–241.

Corson, D. (1997) Critical realism: An emancipatory philosophy for applied linguistics. *Applied Linguistics* 18, 166–188.

Cortazzi, J. and Jin, L. (1996) Culture of learning: Language classroom in China. In H. Coleman (ed.) *Society and the Language Classroom* (pp. 115–134). Cambridge: Cambridge University Press.

Coughlan, P. and Duff, P.A. (1994) Same task, different activities: Analysis of a SLA task from an activity theory perspective. In J.P. Lantolf and G. Appel (eds) *Vygotskian Approaches to Second Language Research* (pp. 173–194). Norwood: Ablex.

Davison, C. and Lai, W. (2007) Competing identities, common issues: Teaching (in) Putonghua. *Language Policy* 6, 119–134.

Dean, K., Joseph, J., Roberts, J.M. and Wight, C. (2006) *Realism, Philosophy and Social Science*. Basingstoke: Palgrave Macmillan.

Deckert, G. (2006) What helped highly proficient EFL learners the most? *TESL Reporter* 39, 1–16.

Donato, R. and McCormick, D. (1994) A sociocultural perspective on language learning strategies: The role of mediation. *The Modern Language Journal* 78, 453–464.

Dörnyei, Z. (2005) *The Psychology of the Language Learner: Individual Differences in Second Language Acquisition.* Mahwah, NJ: Lawrence Erlbaum.

Dörnyei, Z. and Skehan, P. (2003) Individual differences in second language learning. In C.J. Doughty and M.H. Long (eds) *The Handbook of Second Language Acquisition* (pp. 589–630). Malden, MA: Blackwell.

Ehrman, M.E. and Oxford, R.L. (1989) Effects of sex differences, career choice, and psychological type on adult language learning strategies. *The Modern Language Journal* 73, 1–13.

Ellis, R. (1994) *The Study of Second Language Acquisition.* Oxford: Oxford University Press.

Ellis, R. (2004) Individual differences in second language learning. In A. Davies and C. Elder (eds) *The Handbook of Applied Linguistics* (pp. 525–550). Oxford: Blackwell Publishing.

Elman, B. (2000) *A Cultural History of Civil Examinations in Late Imperial China.* Berkley: University of California Press.

Erickson, F. (2004) Demystifying data construction and analysis. *Anthropology and Education Quarterly* 35, 486–493.

Evans, S. (2000) Hong Kong's new English language policy in education. *World Englishes* 19, 185–204.

Fan, M.Y. (2003) Frequency of use, perceived usefulness, and actual usefulness of second language vocabulary strategies: A study of Hong Kong learners. *The Modern Language Journal* 87, 222–241.

Flowerdew, J., Li, D.C.S. and Tran, S. (2002) Discriminatory news discourse: Some Hong Kong data. *Discourse and Society* 13, 319–345.

Fung, A. (2001) What makes the local? A brief consideration of the rejuvenation of Hong Kong identity. *Cultural Studies* 15, 591–601.

Gan, Z., Humphreys, G. and Hamp-Lyons, L. (2004) Understanding successful and unsuccessful EFL students in Chinese universities. *The Modern Language Journal* 88, 229–244.

Gao, X. (2003) Changes in Chinese learners' learner strategy use after arrival in the UK: A qualitative enquiry. In D. Palfreyman and R.C. Smith (eds) *Learner Autonomy across Cultures: Language Education Perspectives* (pp. 41–57). Basingstoke: Palgrave Macmillan.

Gao, X. (2004) A critical review of questionnaire use in learner strategy research. *Prospect, An Australian Journal of TESOL* 19 (3), 3–14.

Gao, X. (2006a) Understanding changes in Chinese students' uses of learning strategies in China and Britain: A socio-cultural re-interpretation. *System* 34, 55–67.

Gao, X. (2006b) Strategies used by Chinese parents to support English language learning: Voices of 'elite' university students. *RELC Journal* 34, 285–298.

Gao, X. (2008a) You had to work hard 'Cause you didn't know whether you were going to wear shoes or straw sandals! *Journal of Language, Identity and Education* 8, 169–187.

Gao, X. (2008b) Shifting motivational discourses among mainland Chinese students in an English medium tertiary institution in Hong Kong: A longitudinal inquiry. *Studies in Higher Education* 33, 599–614.

Gao, X. and Benson, P. (2008) Situating student approaches to learning English in a Chinese context: A re-interpretation of two tertiary vocational learners' experiences. *Asian Journal of English Language Teaching* 18, 41–66.

Gao, X., Cheng, H. and Kelly, P. (2008) Supplementing an uncertain investment? Chinese alliances for English language learning. *Journal of Asia Pacific Communication* 18, 9–29.

Gao, Y., Su, X. and Zhou, L. (2000) Pre-handover language attitudes in Hong Kong, Beijing, and Guangzhou. *Journal of Asian Pacific Communication* 10, 135–153.

Gao, Y., Zhao, Y., Cheng, Y. and Zhou, Y. (2004) Motivation types of Chinese university undergraduates. *Asian Journal of English Language Teaching* 14, 45–64.

Gao, Y., Zhao, Y., Cheng, Y. and Zhou, Y. (2007) Relationships between English learning motivation types and self-identity changes among Chinese students. *TESOL Quarterly* 41, 133–155.

Geertz, C. (1973) *The Interpretation of Cultures: Selected Essays*. New York: Basic Books.

Geertz, C. (1988) *Works and Lives: The Anthropologist as Author*. Stanford: Stanford University Press.

Giddens, A. (1976) *New Rules of Sociological Method: A Positive Critique of Interpretative Sociologies*. London: Hutchinson.

Giddens, A. (1982) *Profiles and Critiques in Social Theory.* London: Macmillan.

Giddens, A. (1984) *The Constitution of Society: Outline of Theory of Structuration*. Berkeley, CA: University of California Press.

Gillette, B. (1994) The role of learner goals in L2 success. In J.P. Lantolf and G. Appel (eds) *Vygotskian Approaches to Second Language Research* (pp. 195–214). Norwood: Ablex.

Goh, C.C.M. (1998) How ESL learners with different listening abilities use comprehension strategies and tactics. *Language Teaching Research* 2, 124–147.

Goh, C.C.M. and Kwah, P.F. (1997) Chinese ESL students' learning strategies: A look at frequency, proficiency and gender. *Hong Kong Journal of Applied Linguistics* 2 (1), 39–53.

Griffiths, C. (2003) Patterns of language learning strategy use. *System* 31, 367–383.

Griffiths, C. (2004) Language learning strategies: Theory and research. Occasional Paper No.1, School of Foundations Studies, Auckland Institute of Studies at St Helens.

Gu, Q. and Brooks, J. (2008) Beyond the accusation of plagiarism. *System* 36, 337–352.

Gu, Y. (2003) Fine brush and freehand: The vocabulary-learning art of two successful Chinese EFL learners. *TESOL Quarterly* 37, 73–104.

Gu, Y. and Johnson, R.K. (1996) Vocabulary learning strategies and language learning outcomes. *Language Learning* 46, 643–679.

Harrison, J., MacGibbon, L. and Morton, M. (2001) Regimes of trustworthiness in qualitative research: The rigors of reciprocity. *Qualitative Inquiry* 6, 323–345.

Harkalau, L. (2005) Ethnography and ethnographic research on second language teaching and learning. In E. Hinkel (ed.) *Handbook of Research in Second Language Teaching and Learning* (pp. 179–194). Mahwah, NJ: Lawrence Erlbaum.

He, A. (2002) Learning English in different linguistic and socio-cultural contexts. *Hong Kong Journal of Applied Linguistics* 7 (2), 107–121.

He, A. (2005) English language teaching in China. In G. Braine (ed.) *Teaching English to the World: History, Curriculum, and Practice* (pp. 11–21). Mahwah, NJ: Lawrence Erlbaum.

HKU Post (2006) The university's internationalization strategy attracts wide attention. *HKU Post* 18, 4.

Ho, D.Y.F., Chau, A.W.L., Chiu, C. and Peng, S.Q. (2003) Ideological orientation and political transition in Hong Kong: Confidence in the future. *Political Psychology* 24, 403–413.

Ho, J. and Crookall, D. (1995) Breaking with Chinese cultural traditions: Learner autonomy in English language teaching. *System* 23, 235–243.

Hsiao, T. and Oxford, R.L. (2002) Comparing theories of language learning strategies: A confirmatory factor analysis. *The Modern Language Journal* 86, 368–383.

Hu, G. (2002a) Recent important developments in secondary English-language teaching in the People's Republic of China. *Language, Culture and Curriculum* 15, 30–49.

Hu, G. (2002b) Potential cultural resistance to pedagogical imports: The case of communicative language teaching in China. *Language, Culture and Curriculum* 15, 93–105.

Hu, G. (2003) English language teaching in China: Regional differences and contributing factors. *Journal of Multilingual and Multicultural Development* 24, 290–318.

Hu, G. (2005) Contextual influences on instructional practices: A Chinese case for an ecological approach to ELT. *TESOL Quarterly* 39, 635–660.

Hu, J. (2004) *The Report for Employment of Graduates*. Beijing: China Compilation and Translation Press.

Hu, X. (2004) Why China English should stand alongside British, American, and the other 'world Englishes'. *English Today* 78 (20.2), 26–33.

Hu, X. (2005) China English, at home and in the world. *English Today* 83 (21.3), 25–35.

Huang, J. (2006) Situated development and use of language learning strategies: EFL learners' perspectives. *Research Studies in Education* 4, 183–197.

Hurd, S. and Lewis, T. (2008) *Language Learning Strategies in Independent Settings*. Bristol: Multilingual Matters.

Jacks, S. (2005) Li Yu Chun loved for being herself. *Time (International Edition)* 166 (15), 56. On WWW at http://www.time.com/time/asia/2005/heroes/li_yuchun.html. Accessed 26.02.2007.

Jiang, Y. (2003) English as a Chinese language. *English Today* 74 (19.2), 3–8.

Jiaoyu Shewai Jianguang Xinxi Wang (Overseas Education Monitor), Ministry of Education (2006) Statistics of Chinese students studying abroad in 2005 (June 6). On WWW at http://www.jsj.edu.cn/dongtai/041.htm. Accessed 26.02.2007.

Jones, J. (1995) Self-access and culture: Retreating from autonomy. *ELT Journal* 49, 228–234.

Keane, M. (2006) From made in China to created in China. *International Journal of Cultural Studies* 9, 285–296.

Kember, D. (2000) Misconceptions about the learning approaches, motivation and study practices of Asian students. *Higher Education* 40, 99–121.

Keung, M.L. (2006) Expressing cultural identities: University students' attitudes towards the use of Putonghua in Hong Kong. Unpublished PhD thesis, University of Leicester, UK.

Kincheloe, J.L. and Berry, K.S. (2004) *Rigour and Complexity in Educational Research: Conceptualizing the Bricolage*. Maidenhead: Open University Press.

Krefting, L. (1991) Rigor in qualitative research: The assessment of trustworthiness. *The American Journal of Occupational Therapy* 45, 214–222.

Lai, M. (2001) Hong Kong students' attitudes towards Cantonese, Putonghua and English after the change of sovereignty. *Journal of Multilingual and Multicultural Development* 22, 112–133.

Lam, W.Y.K. (2009) Examining the effects of metacognitive strategy instruction on ESL group discussions: A synthesis of approaches. *Language Teaching Research* 13 (2), 129–150.

Lan, R. and Oxford, R.L. (2003) Language learning strategy profiles of elementary school students in Taiwan. *International Review of Applied Linguistics in Language Teaching* 41, 339–379.

Lantolf, J. (2000) *Sociocultural Theory and Second Language Learning*. New York: Cambridge University Press.

Lantolf, J. and Appel, G. (eds) (1994) *Vygotskian Approaches to Second Language Research*. Norwood: Ablex.

Lantolf, J. and Thorne, S. (2006) *Sociocultural Theory and the Genesis of L2 Development*. Oxford: Oxford University Press.

Lave, J. and Wenger, E. (1991) *Situated Learning: Legitimate Peripheral Participation*. New York: Cambridge University Press.

Lawson, M.J. and Hogben, D. (1996) The vocabulary learning strategies of foreign language students. *Language Learning* 46, 101–135.

Layder, D. (1981) *Structure, Interaction and Social Theory*. London: Routledge & Kegan Paul.

Layder, D. (1985) Power, structure and agency. *Journal for the Theory of Social Behavior* 15, 131–149.

Layder, D. (1990) *The Realist Image in Social Science*. Basingstoke: Macmillan Press.

Layder, D. (1993) *New Strategies in Social Science Research: An Introduction and Guide*. Cambridge: Polity Press.

Lee, W. (1996) The cultural context for Chinese learners: Conceptions of learning in the Confucian tradition. In D.A. Watkins and J.B. Biggs (eds) *The Chinese Learner: Cultural, Psychological and Contextual Influences* (pp. 25–42). Hong Kong: Comparative Education Research Centre.

Lee, H.C. (2000) *Education in Traditional China: A History*. Leiden: Brill.

Li, F.L.N., Jowett, A.J., Findlay, A.M. and Skeldon, R.S. (1995) Discourse on immigration and ethnic identity: Interviews with professionals in Hong Kong. *Transactions of the Institute of British Geographers* 20, 342–356.

Li, M. (2006) Cross-border higher education of mainland Chinese students: Hong Kong and Macao in a globalizing market. Unpublished doctoral thesis, The University of Hong Kong.

Li, M. and Bray, M. (2007) Cross-border flows of students for higher education: Push–pull factors and motivations of mainland Chinese students in Hong Kong and Macau. *Higher Education* 53, 791–818.

Li, S. and Munby, H. (1996) Meta-cognitive strategies in second language academic reading: A qualitative investigation. *English for Specific Purposes* 15, 199–216.

Littlewood, W. (1999) Defining and developing autonomy in East Asian contexts. *Applied Linguistics* 20, 71–94.

Littlewood, W. (2004) Second language learning theories. In A. Davies and C. Elder (eds) *The Handbook of Applied Linguistics* (pp. 501–524). Oxford: Blackwell Publishing.

LoCastro, V. (1994) Learning Strategies and learning environments. *TESOL Quarterly* 28, 409–414.

Ma, E.K.W. and Fung, A.Y.H. (1999) Re-sinicization, nationalism and the Hong Kong identity. In S. Clement and J. Chan (eds) *Press and Politics in Hong Kong: Case Studies from 1967 to 1997* (pp. 497–528). Hong Kong: Chinese University Press.

Macaro, E. (2006) Strategies for language learning and for language use: Revising the theoretical framework. *The Modern Language Journal* 90, 320–337.

Macaro, E. and Erler, L. (2008) Raising the achievement of young-beginner readers of French through strategy instruction. *Applied Linguistics* 29, 90–109.

McCafferty, S.G., Roebuck, R.F. and Wayland, R.P. (2001) Activity theory and the incidental learning of second language vocabulary. *Language Awareness* 10, 289–294.

McDonough, S.H. (1999) Learner strategies. *Language Teaching* 32, 1–18.

Merriam, S.B. (1988) *Case Study Research in Education: A Qualitative Approach*. San Francisco: Jossey-Bass.

Ming Pao on Friday (2006a) Mainland applicants to Hong Kong's universities increase dramatically. On WWW at http://hk.news.yahoo.com/060616/12/1ouin. html. Accessed 16.06.06.

Ming Pao on Tuesday (2006b) Editorial. 爭尖子大勢所趨 但須爭之有道. On WWW at http://hk.news.yahoo.com/060724/12/1qf52.html. Accessed 25.07.06.

Mistar, J. (2001) English learning strategies of Indonesian university students across individual differences. *Asian Journal of English Language Teaching* 11, 19–44.

Mitchell, R. and Myles, F. (1998) *Second Language Learning Theories*. London: Arnold.

Miyazaki, I. (1976) *China's Examination Hell: The Civil Service Examinations of Imperial China*. New York: Weatherhill.

Morgan, B. (2007) Poststructuralism and applied linguistics: Complementary approaches to identity and culture in ELT. In J. Cummings and C. Davison (eds) *International Handbook of English Language Teaching* (Vol. II, pp. 1033–1052). New York: Springer.

Morrison, K. and Lui, I. (2000) Ideology, linguistic capital and medium of instruction in Hong Kong. *Journal of Multilingual and Multicultural Development* 21, 471–486.

Nassaji, H. (2003) L2 vocabulary learning from context: Strategies, knowledge sources, and their relationship with success in L2 lexical inferencing. *TESOL Quarterly* 37, 645–670.

Ng, C. and Tang, E. (1977) Teachers' needs in the process of EFL reform in China: A report from Shanghai. *Perspectives, City University of Hong Kong, English Department, Working Papers* 9, 63–85.

Norton Peirce, B. (1995) Social identity, investment, and language learning. *TESOL Quarterly* 29, 9–31.

Norton, B. (2000) *Identity and Language Learning: Gender, Ethnicity and Educational Change*. Harlow, England: Longman/Pearson Education.

Norton, B. and Toohey, K. (2001) Changing perspectives on good language learners. *TESOL Quarterly* 35, 307–321.

Norton, B. and Toohey, K. (2004) *Critical Pedagogies and Language Learning*. Cambridge: Cambridge University Press.

Nunan, D. (2003) The impact of English as a global language on educational policies and practices in the Asia-Pacific region. *TESOL Quarterly* 37, 589–614.

Nyikos, M. and Oxford, R.L. (1993) A factor analytic study of language-learning strategy use: Interpretations from information-processing theory and social psychology. *The Modern Language Journal* 77, 11–22.

O'Malley, J.M. and Chamot, A.U. (1990) *Learning Strategies in Second Language Acquisition*. New York: Cambridge University Press.

Oxford, R.L. (1989) Use of language learning strategies: A synthesis of studies with implications for strategy training. *System* 17, 235–247.

Oxford, R.L. (1990) *Language Learning Strategies: What Every Teacher Should Know*. New York: Newbury House/Harper & Row.

Oxford, R.L. (1993) Research on second language learning strategies. *Annual Review of Applied Linguistics* 13, 175–187.

Oxford, R.L. (1996) Why is culture important for language learning strategies? In R.L. Oxford (ed.) *Language Learning Strategies around the World: Cross-Cultural Perspectives* (preface) (Technical Report no. 13). Honolulu: University of Hawaii, Second Language Teaching & Curriculum Center.

Oxford, R.L. (2003) Towards a more systematic model of L2 learner autonomy. In D. Palfreyman and R.C. Smith (eds) *Learner Autonomy across Cultures: Language Education Perspectives* (pp. 75–92). Basingstoke: Palgrave Macmillan.

Oxford, R.L. and Burry-Stock, J.A. (1995) Assessing the use of language learning strategies worldwide with the ESL/EFL version of the strategy inventory for language learning (SILL). *System* 23, 1–23.

Oxford, R.L. and Crookall, D. (1989) Research on language learning strategies: Methods, findings, and instructional issues. *The Modern Language Journal* 73, 404–419.

Oxford, R.L. and Nyikos, M. (1989) Variables affecting choice of language learning strategies by university students. *The Modern Language Journal* 73, 291–300.

Oxford, R.L., Lavine, R.Z., Felkins, G., Hollaway, M.E. and Saleh, A. (1996) Telling their stories: Language students use diaries and recollection. In R.L. Oxford (ed.) *Language Learning Strategies around the World: Cross-Cultural Perspectives* (pp. 19–34) (Technical Report no. 13). Honolulu: University of Hawaii, Second Language Teaching & Curriculum Center.

Oxford, R.L., Cho, Y., Leung, S. and Kim, H. (2004) Effects of the presence and difficulty of task on strategy use: An exploratory study. *International Review of Applied Linguistics in Language Teaching* 42, 1–47.

Palfreyman, D. (2003) Expanding the discourse on learner development: A reply to Anita Wenden. *Applied Linguistics* 24, 243–248.

Palfreyman, D. (2006) Social context and resources for language learning. *System* 34, 352–370.

Parks, S. and Raymond, P.M. (2004) Strategy use by non-native English speaking students in an MBA program: Not business as usual. *The Modern Language Journal* 88, 374–389.

Patton, M.Q. (1990) *Qualitative Evaluation and Research Methods* (2nd edn). Newbury Park, CA: Sage.

Peacock, M. and Ho, B. (2003) Student language learning strategies across eight disciplines. *International Journal of Applied Linguistics* 13, 179–200.

Pennycook, A. (1994) *The Cultural Politics of English as an International Language*. Harlow: Pearson Education.

Phakiti, A. (2003) A closer look at gender and strategy use in L2 reading. *Language Learning* 53, 649–702.

Phelps, L. (2005) Academic achievement of Children in China: The 2002 Fulbright experience. *Psychology in Schools* 42, 233–239.

Phillipson, R. (1992) *Linguistic Imperialism*. Oxford: Oxford University Press.

Pole, C. and Morrison, M. (2003) *Ethnography for Education*. Maidenhead: Open University Press.

Polkinghorne, D.E. (1995) Narrative configuration in qualitative analysis. In J.A. Hatch and R. Wisniewski (eds) *Life History and Narrative* (pp. 5–23). London: Falmer.

Postiglione, G. (2005) Editor's introduction. *Chinese Education and Society* 38 (4), 3–10.

Pritchard, R.M.O. and Maki, H. (2006) The changing self-perceptions of Japanese university students of English. *Journal of Studies in International Education* 10, 141–156.

Putnam, R.D. (2000) *Bowling Alone: The Collapse and Revival of American community*. New York: Simon and Schuster.

Ramanathan, V. and Atkinson, D. (1999) Ethnographic approaches and methods in L2 writing research: A critical guide and review. *Applied Linguistics* 20, 44–70.

Rao, Z. (2006) Understanding Chinese students' use of language learning strategies from cultural and educational perspectives. *Journal of Multilingual and Multicultural Development* 27, 491–508.

Richards, K. (2003) *Qualitative Inquiry in TESOL*. Basingstoke: Palgrave Macmillan.

Ross, H. (1993) *China Learns English: Language Teaching and Social Changes in the People's Republic of China*. New Haven: Yale University Press.

Schack, T. and Schack, E. (2005) In- and outgroup representation in a dynamic society: Hong Kong after 1997. *Asian Journal of Social Psychology* 8, 123–137.

Schulte, B. (2003) Social hierarchy and group solidarity: The meanings of work and vocation/profession in the Chinese context and their implications for vocational education. *International Review of Education* 49, 213–239.

Sealey, A. and Carter, B. (2004) *Applied linguistics as social science*. London: Continuum.

Skyrme, G. (2007) Entering the university: The differentiated experience of two Chinese international students in a New Zealand university. *Studies in Higher Education* 32, 357–372.

Smeyers, P. and Verhesschen, P. (2001) Narrative analysis as philosophical research: Bridging the gap between the empirical and the conceptual. *International Journal of Qualitative Studies in Education* 14, 71–84.

So, D.W.C. (1998) One country, two cultures and three languages: Sociolinguistic conditions and language education in Hong Kong. In B. Asker (ed.) *Teaching Language and Culture: Building Hong Kong on Education* (pp. 152–175). Hong Kong: Addison Wesley Longman.

Sonali, S. (2006) Sharing the world: The researcher and the researched. *Qualitative Research* 5, 207–22.

Stephens, K. (1997) Cultural stereotyping and intercultural communication: Working with students from the People's Republic of China in the UK. *Language and Education* 11, 113–124.

Stevenson, H.W. and Stigler, J.W. (1992) *The Learning Gap: Why Our Schools Are Failing and What We Can Learn from Japanese and Chinese Education*. New York: Touchstone.

Strauss, A. and Corbin, J. (1998) *Basics of Qualitative Research: Techniques and Procedures for Developing Grounded Theory* (2nd edn). London: Sage.

Tan, W. and Simpson, K. (2008) Overseas educational experience of Chinese students. *Journal of Research in International Education* 7 (1) 93–112.

Thøgersen, S. (2002) *A County of Culture: Twentieth-Century China Seen from the Village Schools of Zouping, Shangdong.* Ann Arbor: The University of Michigan Press.

Thorne, S. (2005) Epistemology, politics, and ethics in sociocultural theory. *The Modern Language Journal* 89, 393–409.

Tillman-Healy, L.M. (2003) Friendship as method. *Qualitative Inquiry* 9, 739–749.

Tolstoy, L. (1991) *War and Peace.* Oxford: Oxford University Press.

Toohey, K. and Norton, B. (2003) Learner autonomy as agency in sociocultural settings. In D. Palfreyman and R.C. Smith (eds) *Learner Autonomy across Cultures: Language Education Perspectives* (pp. 58–74). Basingstoke: Palgrave Macmillan.

Tseng, W., Dörnyei, Z. and Schmitt, N. (2006) A new approach to assess strategic learning: The case of self-regulation in vocabulary acquisition. *Applied Linguistics* 27, 78–102.

Tsui, A.B.M. (2004) Language policies in Asian countries: Issues and tensions. *The Journal of Asia TEFL* 1 (2), 1–24.

Watkins, D. (2000) Learning and teaching: A cross-cultural perspective. *School Leadership and Management* 20, 160–173.

Watkins, D. and Biggs, J.B. (1996) *The Chinese Learner: Cultural, Psychological and Contextual Influences.* Hong Kong: Comparative Education Research Centre.

Watson-Gegeo, K.A. (1988) Ethnography in ESL: Defining the essentials. *TESOL Quarterly* 22, 575–592.

Watson-Gegeo, K.A. (2004) Mind, language, and epistemology. *The Modern Language Journal* 88, 331–487.

Wen, W.P. and Clement, R. (2003) A Chinese conceptualisation of willingness to communicate in ESL. *Language, Culture and Curriculum* 16, 18–38.

Wenden, A. (1987) *Learner Strategies in Language Learning.* London: Prentice-Hall International.

Wenden, A. (1998) Metacognitive knowledge and language learning. *Applied Linguistics* 19, 515–537.

Wenden, A. (2002) Learner development in language learning. *Applied Linguistics* 23, 32–55.

Wenger, E. (1998) *Community of Practice: Learning, Meaning, and Identity.* New York: Cambridge University Press.

Wenger, E. (2000) Communities of practice and social learning systems. *Organization* 7, 225–246.

Wolcott, H. (1995) Making a study 'more ethnographic'. In J. Van Maanen (ed.), *Representation in ethnography* (pp. 79–111). London: Sage.

Yang, F. (2002) Education in China. *Educational Philosophy and Theory* 34, 135–144.

Yang, N. (1999) The relationship between EFL learners' beliefs and learning strategy use. *System* 27, 515–535.

Yin, R. (1994) *Case Study Research: Design and Methods* (2nd ed.). Thousand Oaks, CA: Sage.

Yu, X. (2004, November 15) 三年跳过四道难关　克服出国 "水土不服. *Beijing Morning.* On WWW at http://news.xinhuanet.com/overseas/2004-11/15/content_2219389.htm. Accessed 26.02.2006.

Zhang, J.L. (2003) Research into Chinese EFL learner strategies: Methods, findings and instructional issues. *RELC Journal* 34, 284–322.

Zhao, J. and Guo, J. (2002) The restructuring of China's higher education: An experience for market economy and knowledge economy. *Educational Philosophy and Theory* 34, 207–221.

Zhao, Y. and Campbell, K.P. (1995) English in China. *World Englishes* 14, 377–390.

Zuengler, J. and Miller, E.R. (2006) Cognitive and sociocultural perspectives: Two parallel SLA worlds. *TESOL Quarterly* 40, 35–58.

Index

Skeldon, R.S. 38, 109, 121
Skyrme, G. 4, 116
Smeyers, P. 4, 43
Sociocultural perspectives on language
  learning 4, 9-32, 100, 151-159
– memorization 46, 47, 49, 50, 52, 63, 65-67,
  77, 78, 90, 97, 104, 105, 111, 112, 122-124,
  126, 132, 137, 139, 140, 146, 147
– socialization (*also* socialization process
  and socializing with other learners) 40,
  58, 76, 101, 103, 104, 108, 113, 119, 121,
  125, 129-131, 140, 144, 147, 155, 156
– strategy use 46-53, 76, 86-91, 117-124,
  125-132, 133-139, 140-148
Strauss, A. 6, 43, 85
Structure and agency debate 25-30
– agency 3, 7-10, 19-21, 23, 24, 25-30, 41,
  75-80, 89, 110, 111-114, 116, 118, 120, 124,
  127, 132, 139, 145, 148, 149, 152, 154-161
– realist position 26, 28-30
– structuralist position 26-27
– structuration position 26, 28
– structure (*also* contextual conditions and

context) 7-9, 10, 18-20, 25-32, 41, 75,
  77-80, 110, 111, 113, 114, 129, 132, 139,
  148-152, 155-151
– voluntarist position 26-27

Thorne, S. 2, 9, 17, 19, 20, 75
Thøgersen, S. 33, 34, 53, 54, 57, 68, 73, 78,
  82, 100, 109
Toohey, K. 2, 4, 17, 19, 20, 25, 27, 120, 153,
  155,
Tseng, W. 2, 11, 16, 26, 53, 155, 158

Verhesschen, P. 4, 43

Watkins, D. 47, 58
Watson-Gegeo, K.A. 2, 4, 17, 19, 20
Wenden, A. 2, 10, 23, 24, 64, 154, 158
Wenger, E. 18-20, 58

Yang, N. 15, 53, 77, 159

Zhang, L.J. 2, 9, 11
Zuengler, J. 2, 4, 9, 17, 19, 153, 157